I have known my good ⟨...⟩ and I can still clearly re⟨...⟩ York. There's one reason I can recall that today: because even then Joe was helping me improve and reach higher potential. In his book *The Jesus Principles* he unpacks that with authenticity and transparency. This book is not a theoretic construct, rather who Joe Mattera is—a builder of people.

—SAM CHAND
LEADERSHIP CONSULTANT
AUTHOR, *NEW THINKING, NEW FUTURE*
WWW.SAMCHAND.COM

The hard work of raising up leaders is becoming a lost art. Outsider resumes have become more important than in-house discipleship. I have seen my father raise up leaders for decades, and I constantly share stories of how I have seen this happen. This book expertly distills years of practice into practical wisdom for leaders looking to disciple as Christ did.

—JUSTIN MATTERA
OWNER, MATTERA MANAGEMENT

Most books describe the fruits of behaviors and practices that may work for a season in a particular culture or context. This book goes to the roots that produce these fruits in every generation, culture, and context. This key difference is because this author, Dr. Joseph Mattera, is a globally recognized thought leader, author, practitioner, and seasoned culture shaper who knows the heart of God and the times that we are called to influence. I predict this read will have one of the longest shelf lives in your library because it was built to last.

—DR. JOSEPH UMIDI
EXECUTIVE VICE PRESIDENT, REGENT UNIVERSITY
FOUNDER, LIFEFORMING LEADERSHIP COACHING

I have been deeply encouraged by the ministry and writing of Bishop Mattera. He has a rare combination of deep theological insight, practical ministry, and a pastor's heart. In *The Jesus Principles* he brings this integration together in a profound way. I believe this book, full of truth and wisdom and immensely relevant for our cultural moment, will deepen and equip those serving the church.

—JON TYSON
LEAD PASTOR, CHURCH OF THE CITY NEW YORK
AUTHOR, *THE BURDEN IS LIGHT*

Are you looking for a book to refresh your relationship with Jesus? Do you want to rekindle your fire for following Christ? Are you new to the Christian faith and want to go deeper faster in your growth? *The Jesus Principles* by Dr. Joseph Mattera is an incredible tool in your hand that will help you do all of the above. Dr. Mattera has done it again with this powerful and practical book that will challenge and empower you in your walk with Christ! As a pastor, I want to put a copy of this book in the hands of every longtime member as well as first-time attender of my church (and you will too)! You need to read *The Jesus Principles*, and so does every other Christ follower you know!

—DR. GREG WILLIAMSON
LEAD PASTOR, VALLEY CHRISTIAN CHURCH
PRESIDENT, CONNEXUS LEADERSHIP NETWORK

Bishop Joe has done it again. He has written a book that is both biblically strong and speaking to this present moment of where the church is at and needs to be. *The Jesus Principles* will refocus and release you to get back to the main work of changing the world, which is through authentic relationship and intentional discipleship. This book helps to reclaim the church's true mission, which is a Jesus movement that invests in people rather than programs. This book is both practical and inspirational. I recommend it for pastors, church leaders, marketplace leaders, and all followers of Jesus who want to make disciples.

—JOHN HAMMER
SENIOR PASTOR, SONRISE CHRISTIAN CENTER (ISONRISE.ORG)
COFOUNDER, REPRESENT MOVEMENT
(REPRESENTMOVEMENT.COM)

I was without a spiritual father for four years after my beloved mentor Dr. Elias Malki went to glory. Then our merciful King Yahweh led me to Bishop Joseph Mattera. The knowledge, understanding, and wisdom that flow through him have greatly challenged and enlightened me as a man of God. Bishop Mattera is a twenty-first-century theologian, an authentic apostolic voice—not an echo. It is this unique voice that cries out with impact through every page of this book, "Prepare ye the way of the Lord; make his paths straight" (Matt. 3:3, KJV). The book will lead you from success to significance with a revived passion to become Christlike. Your zeal to abide in the vine will increase, and you will become a disciple indeed. You will know the truth, and the truth will set you free.

—APOSTLE RAFAEL NAJEM
SENIOR PASTOR, CCF MINISTRIES
PRESIDENT, SOMEBODY CARES NEW ENGLAND
PRESIDENT, GREATER LOWELL CITYWIDE MINISTRIES NETWORK

Dr. Joseph Mattera's book, *The Jesus Principles*, is a captivating and motivating blueprint for every individual who desires to unleash the innate potential, passion, and purpose for his or her life.

—Steve Fedyski
CEO, Cloudburst Entertainment

In *The Jesus Principles*, Bishop Joseph Mattera clearly helps us learn not only how to be leaders but how to disciple leaders. This book is good for anyone at any stage of his or her spiritual growth, being conformed into the image of Christ. From years' experience Bishop Mattera excels in sharing biblical truth with personal experience to help us grow into the leaders that God has planned for us, leaders who will advance the kingdom of God. I encourage you not only to read the book but to apply the principles in your life and in the lives of those you are leading. If you are serious about being a disciple and helping others become disciples, this is a must-read.

—Terry Moore
Lead Pastor, Sojourn Church

The Jesus Principles by Joseph Mattera is a book that should be in every leader's library. You will want to read it, then review it over and over again. Mattera uses the Scriptures and his experience to discuss the most important concepts leaders need every day. Starting with identity and following through to attitudes, skills, habits, and especially relationships, he brings these to bear on your life in a very simple and practical way. *The Jesus Principles* will help guide the emerging leader and refresh the established leader. I encourage everyone to read and apply the Jesus principles.

—Dr. Tim Hamon
CEO, Christian International
PhD, Regent University

Bishop Mattera has patiently guided my husband and me through numerous seasons of spiritual discovery. He has done so with grace, intellect, encouragement, and at times correction. As I am a marketplace leader in New York City, our lives are quite diverse. His ability to instantly shift between business and church clearly exemplifies his call to shape culture and speak into what is relevant today. This book offers a fresh synopsis of how one should execute the call of God regardless of where the person is in his or her walk. Bishop seamlessly lays out the church's true mission in a didactic, yet inspirational, way. We are reminded throughout the book that we are one body, under one God, called uniquely and according to His will and His plan to govern the world according to His Word. This book is a keeper!

—KRISTINA HOSCH
CEO, KRISLEN MANAGEMENT
EXECUTIVE DIRECTOR, CHRIST COVENANT COALITION
AND THE REVOLVING DOOR INC.
AUTHOR, #90SECSWITHGOD

JOSEPH MATTERA

The JESUS Principles

CHARISMA
HOUSE

Visit the author's website at http://josephmattera.org/.

Library of Congress Cataloging-in-Publication Data

Names: Mattera, Joseph, author.
Title: The Jesus principles / by Joseph Mattera.
Description: Lake Mary : Charisma House, 2019. | Includes bibliographical references.
Identifiers: LCCN 2019022516 (print) | LCCN 2019022517 (ebook) | ISBN 9781629996271 (trade paperback) | ISBN 9781629996288 (ebook)
Subjects: LCSH: Jesus Christ--Example.
Classification: LCC BT304.2 .M337 2019 (print) | LCC BT304.2 (ebook) | DDC 232.9/04--dc23
LC record available at https://lccn.loc.gov/2019022516
LC ebook record available at https://lccn.loc.gov/2019022517

19 20 21 22 23 — 987654321
Printed in the United States of America

*I dedicate this book to my lovely wife, Joyce,
and my biological and spiritual children as
well as the family of families called
Resurrection Church, in which I learned
how to walk out the Jesus principles.*

Table of Contents

Foreword by Kristian Hernandez........ xv

Introduction..........................xix

Chapter 1 Understanding Your God-Given Identity ...1

Chapter 2 Unleashing Your Potential................9

Chapter 3 Going to Jerusalem 19

Chapter 4 Understanding Affirmation..............35

Chapter 5 Loving and Being Loved 47

Chapter 6 Unleashing Others' Potential.............65

Chapter 7 Walking in Your Assignment 81

Chapter 8 The Power of Failure....................91

Chapter 9 The Power of Delegation 113

Chapter 10 The Power of Prioritizing...............123

Chapter 11 The Power of Community 133

Chapter 12 The Power of Secure Leadership.........141

Chapter 13 Understanding Struggle 153

Chapter 14 Understanding the Future 169

Chapter 15 Understanding Spiritual Authority 175

Chapter 16 The Power of Prayer 185

Chapter 17 Ending Well 193

Chapter 18 Transformational Questions to Ask
Yourself. 201

Appendix Effective Ways to Help Mature Christ
Followers. 207

Notes 227

About the Author 231

Foreword

IF YOU ARE like most ministry leaders I meet, you are likely in a constant search for models of discipleship and leadership development. Perhaps you have tried so many different things that you might even feel tired or cynical toward this subject. If that's you, I'm so glad you are reading this book because it provides insights, real-life examples, and a Christ-centered theology to develop leaders.

The book you are holding has the potential to alter the course of your life, leadership, and ministry. That's a strong claim, but as you turn the pages, I'm confident you will agree with me. It's a rare experience when a book can both broaden your thinking and move your heart. Those kinds of books hold a special place in my library, but books that broaden our thinking, move our hearts, and enhance our ministry skills deserve their own shelf! Those kinds of books are truly priceless, as they wed keen insights with truths that awaken our hearts and practical tools that make our hands effective for God's work.

Though you are just finding out about this book, I've known about this book for over twenty years. I saw this book unfold before my eyes from the moment I came to Christ at the age of fourteen at Bishop Mattera's church, and shortly after, I joined a discipleship group he formed.

The group was called Men in Training (MIT), and this group met Sunday mornings before our corporate worship gatherings. Bishop handpicked these men and called them to a high level of commitment of discipleship and leadership in our church. To my young mind this group was like the Navy SEALs in our church! I wanted to be like these men with every fiber of my being. They were husbands and fathers and leaders in our community, and as a young man who grew up in a single-parent home, my esteem for these men could not have been higher. Given this context, I can't overstate that one of the proudest moments of my young life was when Bishop invited me as a teenager to join this group! He made room for a teenager within a group of men because he saw potential in me and was willing to invest in me for the long haul.

Now, at the age of thirty-nine, married twelve years to my wonderful wife, Erin, enjoying our three kids, and serving as lead pastor of Hope Astoria, I'm amazed that my entire life changed as a result of this one invitation. During those MIT gatherings, Bishop taught us God's

Word, instilled a thirst for the presence of God, and challenged us to grow in character. We were inspired and equipped to grow as leaders in our homes, the church, our businesses, and our careers. I still have the notebooks from those times of teaching and have journals filled with reflections and insights I gained.

As transformative as those classes were, what truly changed my life was when Bishop invited me to live with his family. Living with Bishop and his family was the greatest discipleship opportunity I would ever be offered. I saw how he lived outside of the pulpit, how he loved his wife and cared for his family. We went food shopping together, went on family vacations, and did chores around the house together. We ate meals together, argued and resolved conflicts, and laughed a ton. But I also saw Bishop pray like a man from another planet, devour Scripture, fast for weeks on end, and prioritize family devotions amid a crazy busy life.

What this book provides to leaders and churches is fresh content and vision for our classroom settings, but its true genius is the call to us as leaders to offer our daily lives to create a discipleship culture. Everything you need to develop leaders and unleash human potential in your ministry context is right there under your nose, namely your everyday life. Your home, your chores, your family rhythms, and a thousand other normal situations we walk past every day are potent tools in the hands of God to unleash a discipleship revolution.

The true gift of this book is not only the behind-the-scenes glimpses into the life of a leader we can all learn from, but mainly the way he calls us back to model the life of Jesus. We don't have to reinvent the wheel! Jesus discipled and unleashed human potential better than anyone in history. This book calls us to take a fresh look at our Lord and translate his life and model to our contexts as we learn from the life and ministry of a fruitful leader. Bishop pioneered a church and ministry in one of the most difficult cities in which to do ministry in the world, with no resources, during the crack epidemic of the '80s and '90s. Not only did he disciple poor people, broken people, and people battling addictions; he also discipled people who were educated and had wealth. It was messy, not easy, but armed with the model and life of Jesus, God did amazing things!

May this book spur you to see the potential in yourself and others through redemptive eyes! Take the tools, insights, and inspiration you will find here, and put them into practice. Start somewhere, but please simply start! I'm confident if we do so, we will see God do amazing things over the course of our lives.

—KRISTIAN HERNANDEZ
LEAD PASTOR, HOPE ASTORIA
FOUNDER, THE KERYGMA GROUP
AUTHOR, *BEHOLDING AND PROCLAIMING*

Introduction

*J*ESUS TOLD HIS disciples that the only way to find one's life is to lose it (Mark 8:35)—that life was only worth living if one is willing to die for something greater than one's self. This was only one of the many countercultural teachings of Jesus. His teachings are as controversial today in our American culture as they were to first-century Jewish culture. Yet in the face of great opposition Jesus was able to take twelve men and create the largest, most influential movement the world has ever seen. He lived an extraordinary life and left behind an eternal legacy through His disciples. True influence should increase through the lives of those we pour into, even after we pass away. Our greatest example of this is of course Jesus, whose followers did greater works than He did after His resurrection and ascension.

Jesus never wrote a book and never traveled farther than the general region of Israel where He was born and raised. He had no servants, yet many called Him "Master." He had no degree, yet they called Him "Teacher." He had no medicines, yet they called Him "Healer." He had no army, yet kings feared Him. He won no military battles, yet He conquered the world. He committed no crime, yet they crucified Him. He was buried in a tomb, yet He lives today. Jesus remained steadfast to God the Father's will for His life, never suffering from what I call "mission drift." Mission drift happens when we are caught up in issues that prevent us from reaching our full potential. Our full potential includes unleashing greatness in our spouses, children, friends, and families, thereby leaving a legacy for all future generations. We can do this by following the principles that Jesus used to unleash human potential and turn the world upside down.

This book is an invitation to join me on a journey to release your purpose through the principles of Jesus. Before we begin this journey, I have seven questions for you. Your answers to these questions will serve as indicators of the status of your current purposeful state as well as help you understand the extent to which you are experiencing mission drift. God does not intend for you to live adrift. He intends that you have life, and life abundant—living with purpose so that those who come after you can go forward from the legacy you leave them.

1. Are you experiencing continual frustration?

Continual frustration is one of the most obvious signs you are not walking toward what God has internally wired you to pursue. In fact, your frustration may be a God-given sign to awaken you to the real passion and purpose He has for you. If you are suffering from mission drift, you will be going against the internal impulses from God that give you delight. Going against these internal impulses means you are doing things that do not match your gifts, passion, and grace. If you are struggling with continual frustration, it's time to stop and reflect on the reasons and on how you can come into alignment with God's purpose for your life. Don't waste years going in the wrong direction.

2. Are you suffering burnout?

Another telltale sign you are suffering from mission drift is that you have to work hard at accomplishing things in your own strength. When you do this for too long, you experience burnout. When you are in mission drift, you are not walking in obedience to the Lord. Hence, you are not being sustained by His grace and are instead working merely with fleshly strength. This can soon lead to emotional or spiritual burnout if you don't readjust. Jesus has called you to enter His rest and cease from your own labors (Matt. 11:28–30; Heb. 4:9–11).

3. Is there a lack of fruit in your life?

A person in mission drift does not maximize his or her effectiveness, resulting in a lack of fruit. You are unique and have a calling unlike any other. When you are hitting your sweet spot regarding your calling, you are doing things that few can match, hitting the mark in your purpose and bearing much fruit in the way Jesus called us to do (John 15:8).

4. How do you remain faithful to the original call of God on your life?

Every once in a while I review my prophetic journal to make sure I am still pursuing the original calling God gave me when I first started serving Him more than thirty years ago. The methods may change as I mature, but the mission remains the same since God chose each of us before the foundation of the world and gave us a purpose before we were even born (Eph. 1:4; 2 Tim. 1:9). When you are in mission drift, you have strayed from the original calling God gave you.

5. Do you find yourself losing focus?

Activity does not necessarily result in productivity. Many people are very busy running around focused on minor things and neglecting the primary things God has called them to. I am not saying you should neglect the mundane and ordinary routines of life but rather that you should make sure you prioritize and manage your time within those routines in such a way that the most important things are taken care of first. When you don't prioritize your time, your activities will not match your purpose.

6. How often do you put things before people?

The kingdom of God is built upon relationships, not ministry or work. Everyone is called to invest in key relationships, whether it be immediate family, spiritual children, mentors, or key people you are called to "do life" with. The enemy would love for you to put programs before people, because at the end of the day the only things you will take with you into eternity are people—not programs, real estate, money, or the material things in life. When you have no quality time for those key relationships, then most likely you are suffering from mission drift. You need to proactively pursue those people who are most important to you in life.

7. How good are you at keeping the main thing the main thing?

The enemy of "best" is usually something good. The enemy does not come in a red suit with a pitchfork; he comes as an angel of light. Hence, one of his greatest strategies is to get you so focused on doing something good for God or your family that it blinds you to what is best. To avoid mission drift, you must always keep first things first and keep the main thing the main thing.

As you press in and ponder your responses to these seven questions, I pray that the Holy Spirit convicts you of your need to explore the principles Jesus used to release purpose in His followers. What worked for His disciples will work for you because "Jesus Christ is the same yesterday and today and forever" (Heb. 13:8).

Chapter 1

Understanding Your God-Given Identity

THROUGH MANY DECADES of working with people, I have found that many just cannot figure out who they really are. Often this is because they have spent many years being people pleasers and pretending to be whatever would get them accepted at that moment. I tell them not to worry about who they are but to decide who they want to be and become that person. I remind them that we all have choices and that God promises in Philippians 4:13 that we can do all things if we ask Jesus to give us the strength.

People are often so used to being dominated and controlled that it gives them great relief to realize how much freedom we actually have as Christians. Selfish people resent that Christianity limits their ability to sin, but if you stop and think about it, every sin you could possibly commit hurts somebody. Why would anyone want to go through life using and hurting people? A few years ago I heard the story of a Tom Thumb grocery store clerk who accidentally gave a man twenty dollars too much in change. When the man went back in and returned it, the clerk was very surprised, saying nobody had ever returned money to her before. When she asked him why he returned it, he told her that liking himself for being a good and honest man was worth much more than twenty bucks!

When I began mentoring a young man named Kristian regarding his potential, purpose, and calling, our time together started an internal process of recalibration, causing his identity to gradually change. This was crucial in his life because you must change how you view yourself before you can change your behavior and ultimately unleash your potential and achieve your purpose. While you were growing up, your self-image may have been tarnished by negative words spoken over you, whether at home with your parents and siblings or at school with your friends and class-mates. Your name may be Joe or John, Susan or Christine, but inside you may really think your name is "jerk," "idiot," "failure," or "fool." The negative words others have spoken over you have branded you with a negative identity that has more clout and influence than the name on your birth cer-tificate. The power of the words spoken over a life cannot be overstated. Proverbs 18:21 teaches that "death and life are in the power of the tongue."

Receive Your New Name

One of the most significant things that must take place in order for your human potential to be unleashed is your internal "name" must be changed. Your choice to follow Christ and overcome the temptations of the flesh brings you to a place where Jesus can give you a new name. This is why one of the first things Jesus did to unleash Peter's potential was change his name from his birth name, Simon, to his divine name, Peter, which means rock or stone.[1] In Matthew 16:18 we see this process expanded even more when Jesus said He would build His church upon this rock, or *petra*. The word *petra* in this context refers to a large, immovable rock.[2] Jesus changed Peter's name so that his self-image would equal the unique calling on his life and unleash his vast human potential to establish the church as the body of Christ.

We also see this principle powerfully illustrated in the story of the great patriarch Abraham. When God changed his name from Abram, which merely means "exalted father," to Abraham, or "father of a multitude,"[3] it unleashed his faith so his destiny of blessing the nations could be realized. He had to go from knowing himself as a father to understanding that God intended him to be a father of many nations, even though he and his wife, Sarai (Sarah), were old and barren with no natural possibility of having children. I can just picture this childless, ninety-nine-year-old man commanding his more than three hundred servants and his barren wife to call him by his God-given identity even though it looked foolish in the light of his current conditions!

Romans 4:16–22 says Abraham was able to do this by not considering "his own body, which was as good as dead," or the deadness of Sarah's womb but by believing and speaking what God's Word said about them instead of how the natural world saw them. When Abraham accepted his name change and believed what God said, he and Sarah were able to have the child of promise even though he was one hundred years old and Sarah was past childbearing age.

In 2 Corinthians the apostle Paul warns us to regard people based on their divine identity and not on their fleshly or earthly identity.

> Consequently, from now on we estimate and regard no one from a [purely] human point of view [in terms of natural standards of value]. [No] even though we once did estimate Christ from a human viewpoint and as a man, yet now [we have such knowledge of Him that] we know Him no longer [in terms of the flesh]. Therefore if any person is [ingrafted] in Christ (the Messiah) he is a new creation (a new creature altogether); the old [previous moral and spiritual condition] has passed away. Behold, the fresh and new has come!
> —2 CORINTHIANS 5:16–17, AMPC

Saul persecuted Christians because he judged Jesus and His followers according to the flesh, like any other human being. After his conversion Saul received his new name, Paul, and his new identity that unleashed not only *his* human potential but that of untold millions of people years beyond his natural lifetime.

When I saw Kristian walk into our church, I didn't see a fatherless, purposeless Hispanic teenager; I saw an emerging leader with the potential to be a world changer. I also knew I was assigned to mentor him and unleash his potential; therefore, I spoke to his God-given identity, which helped him develop into the image of Christ right before my eyes! The great news about salvation is that when you give your life to Christ, you become a new creation—the old has passed away, and all things have become new. Even though your physical appearance may remain the same, your true identity instantly changes as God begins to reveal His divine purpose and calling for your life! Revelation 2:17 promises that Jesus "will give him a white stone, with a new name written on the stone that no one knows except the one who receives it." This will be a special, secret new name that only Jesus and you will understand.

To unleash potential in others, we need to stop judging people according to the flesh and begin to see people with the eyes of God. In the natural I may see a person who is a drunkard or a drug addict, homeless or impoverished, depressed or a failure in business. Yet as a believer I am called to see every individual with his God-given identity so his name can be changed, his self-image repaired, and his vast human potential unleashed! As a leader I am especially called to cast vision to those I serve by bringing to their mind's eye a sense of their future to motivate them to begin to unleash their potential starting today.

Cultivate Your Spiritual Life

I have found that the most important habit I can help instill in others to release their potential is to meditate on the Word of God. Scripture teaches that personal transformation only comes when the mind is renewed (Rom. 12:1–2). Although you are a new creation when you are born from above (2 Cor. 5:17), your mind and emotions have to undergo a process of reprogramming your pattern of thinking, which can take many years. This is not for salvation but for maturity and sanctification.

Only the Word of God can cleanse and rewire the human mind so that it is sanctified (John 17:17). Only by thinking Christ's thoughts after Him can you break the strongholds that put you in internal prisons and limit your growth capacity (2 Cor. 10:3–5). Only by knowing and understanding the Word of God can you understand when thoughts, ideas, concepts, and paradigms you have embraced have limited you. It is only by the Word of Christ that you can command these thoughts and concepts to loosen their grip on you!

This is why the apostle Paul told the Philippian church that the key to breaking anxiety and walking in peace was to cultivate the spiritual life (Phil. 4:6–7) and walk in a pattern of healthy thinking: "Finally, brothers and sisters, whatever is true, whatever is noble, whatever is right, whatever is pure, whatever is lovely, whatever is admirable—if anything is excellent or praiseworthy—think about such things" (Phil.

4:8, NIV). Psychologists today know the science behind what Paul is writing here. A *Psychology Today* article notes:

> Every thought releases brain chemicals. Being focused on negative thoughts effectively saps the brain of its positive forcefulness, slows it down, and can go as far as dimming your brain's ability to function, even creating depression. On the flip side, thinking positive, happy, hopeful, optimistic, joyful thoughts decreases cortisol and produces serotonin, which creates a sense of well-being. This helps your brain function at peak capacity.[4]

The article also notes that "negative thinking slows down brain coordination, making it difficult to process thoughts and find solutions." Fear affects activity in the cerebellum, slowing down "the brain's ability to process new information—limiting your ability to practice creative problem solving." Your thoughts can also "potentially rewire your brain by creating stronger neuronal pathways and synapses. What you think and feel about a certain situation or thing can become so deeply ingrained that you will have to work hard to dismantle the negative connections and rewire your brain in order to be less afraid, to think positively, to believe that dreams can come true, to trust that your efforts will be successful."[5]

Meditate on the Word of God

When God called Joshua to take Moses' place as the leader of the nation of Israel, He told him that the key to his success was to meditate and speak out the written Word of the Lord. He instructed him, "This book of the law shall not depart from your mouth, but you shall meditate on it day and night, so that you may be careful to do according to all that is written in it; for then you will make your way prosperous, and then you will have success" (Josh. 1:8, NASB). The command given to Joshua to meditate had to do with muttering the divine words, thinking the words, and ruminating on the words in his heart so that he would be able to view both himself and the world the way God does in order to fulfill his divine assignment.

The psalmist said of God, "Your word I have treasured in my heart, that I may not sin against You" (Ps. 119:11, NASB). In another place he said, "Your word is a lamp to my feet and a light to my path" (Ps. 119:105, NASB). The apostle Paul, in his mentoring of his protégé Timothy, exhorted him to continue learning the Scriptures, which would give him wisdom in salvation since "all Scripture is inspired by God and profitable for teaching, for reproof, for correction, for training in righteousness; so that the man of God may be adequate, equipped for every good work (2 Tim. 3:16–17, NASB).

Chapter 2

Unleashing Your Potential

KRISTIAN WAS ONLY fourteen years old when he gave his life to the Lord and started attending our church. His testimony is powerful.

> I was born as the result of an adulterous affair that caused great scandal. My sister was the first to be born of this affair. Her birth caused a huge scandal, and my mom decided that her and my father's relationship should end. My dad refused to let this happen. He would say, "You ruined my life; you can't get out of this that easy. This is over when I say it's over." He would break into her apartment and wait for her at the end of her work shift or harass her all the way home from work. Eventually they were together again, and I was conceived. When my dad found out, he was determined to not let it happen

again, and so he took my mom to the abortion clinic three times. Each time, my mother would lie and say she went through with it. When he would realize she lied to him, he would beat her in order to force a miscarriage. The third time my mother went to the abortion clinic, a woman stopped her in the parking lot and said, "Don't kill this baby. God has a plan for this child," and my mother just broke down and wept. That night she boarded a plane and headed to Puerto Rico with my sister. She gave birth to me in Puerto Rico, and six months after my birth my dad died. I never knew him.

Kris was a typical fatherless young man, living in the rough and tumble streets of Sunset Park in Brooklyn, New York. Although he was raised by a heroic single mother who tried to keep him in line, Kristian still had an emotional void in his life. No matter how capable a mother is, all young men need a father figure to lean upon. I saw vast potential and ability in Kris, and I invited him to live with my family so he could have the influence of a father, not just a Sunday pastor. Through the seven or eight years he lived with us, he became part of the family; he was treated as one of my sons and accepted by my five biological children as their brother.

I did my best to accept Kristian just the way he was and not push him into any particular direction, leaving him and God to figure that out. Within a few years he desired to move into more of a ministry role, so he became one of the church leaders as the assistant to the youth director. At one point I put him in charge of the youth. But after several months he felt he was in over his head, had a slight meltdown, and didn't even show up for services! Rather than quit on him, I realized he had been placed in leadership prematurely, so I put him back as the assistant under the former director of the youth.

At another point in his growth process he actually left New York and moved out of state to live with a minister friend of mine for six months. During this difficult time, I was grieved because I felt he was running away instead of dealing with issues in his life. Thankfully God answered my prayers, and Kristian came back to live with us. A year later, at his request, I put him back in charge of our youth ministry, and he did an amazing job. He stayed as the director of our youth until he handed it over to my youngest son, Justin, whom he helped mentor to take over this ministry.

Soon after, Kristian was appointed as a pastor/director of ministries in our church, and he turned out to be one of the wisest, most balanced, and most gifted young leaders I have ever seen. He began preaching for me when I went away, and he even coached the leaders of our ministries. Eventually he was sent out from our church to help plant a church. He soon thereafter became the lead pastor and key component of a thriving church-planting movement emanating from his local congregation that has resulted in more than a half dozen church plants in just a few years—unheard of in NYC! Truly there are various ebbs and flows in human development and many peaks and valleys involved between those cultivating growth and those they aid in the unleashing of potential. In the case of Kristian and me, all the years of pain and process have been well worth it.[1]

As a pastor and minister since 1984, I have focused most of my time on leadership development. One of the most important aspects of developing leaders—and one of the hardest in the world to accomplish—is getting people to recognize and unleash their God-given human potential. It has been said that the breakfast of champions is not cereal but struggle. Unleashing potential involves understanding and working with a person's natural gifting—his or her unique assignment and particular calling in life, as well as the past experiences that have framed his or her outlook on life. Many of the people who come into our church have come from broken families. The greatest hindrance they have in unleashing and maximizing their gifts and talents is their own fear of failure, often combined with deep-seated feelings of low self-esteem. Past negative experiences and the negative input they have received within key relationships make it difficult for them to believe in themselves.

Getting people to believe in themselves as they begin to discover their God-given abilities is one of the most important and rewarding aspects of helping unleash potential. It is interesting that Jesus, who is the greatest developer of people who ever lived, said His disciples would become fishers of men. *Becoming*, which means changing or developing into something, is a process that every person must go through if he or she is going to unleash potential, though it can often be a long and difficult journey that requires determination and steadfastness.

The Process

I cannot explain why God allows there to be so much pain in this sinful world, but I do know God allowed His own Son, Jesus, to suffer more pain than any other human has ever suffered. As a matter of fact, the Bible says Jesus suffered and was tempted in every way that we could ever possibly encounter. Immediately after Jesus was baptized by John, and God declared Jesus as His Son, in whom He was well pleased, the Holy Spirit led Him into His own wilderness experience. We will each face our own wilderness experience as part of the process to unleash our human potential. How we handle that experience determines the extent to which our potential will be unleashed. God wants us to understand that the process is just as important as the product.

We know that the children of Israel were led through their wilderness experience by God for the express purpose of proving them and exposing what was really in their hearts, not toward God but to each and every one of them. The apostle Paul, who wrote a majority of the New Testament, testified of many difficult and trying wilderness experiences as he traveled throughout Europe and Asia on his many missionary journeys. We know from his powerful letters that God had done a great work in him, changing him from the great persecutor introduced to us in Acts chapter 9 to the inspired author of most of the New Testament epistles. Paul wrote, "I have been crucified with Christ. It is no longer I who live, but Christ who lives in me.

And the life I now live in the flesh I live by faith in the Son of God, who loved me and gave himself for me" (Gal. 2:20).

Regarding the process that brings maturity to a person, many in the body of Christ are in a wilderness experience—even in this day and age. The wilderness is a place in Christ in which you are out of the house of bondage, but you are not quite in the promised land. The promised land is when you are walking in the fullness of the Spirit and of purpose in Christ Jesus. The wilderness is a great time of testing, confusion, and frustration that can bring out the dark side of our souls, because we are constantly confronted with our false self, which manifests the most while we are in the fire. Many saints of old have called this period "the dark night of the soul."

Temptations Common to All

Jesus, as the second Adam, didn't sin in the midst of temptation even when He was hungry and in the wilderness. This contrasts with the first Adam, who sinned by eating the forbidden fruit while in paradise with all his needs being met. There are four main temptations every one of us goes through based on the epic contest between Satan and Jesus when He was in the wilderness, as seen in the Gospel narratives (Luke 4:1–13). Let's look at each one individually.

Temptation 1: "If you are the Son of God" = the test of identity

One of the greatest tests in the wilderness is when we begin to doubt our identity in Christ. Satan said to Jesus,

"If you are the Son of God..." (Luke 4:1, emphasis added). When we are in times of great tests and trials, the enemy tries to get us to doubt our salvation, our place in Christ as His child, and even the reality of Christianity. If he can cause us to lose our identity, then he can frame another identity for us. For instance, our culture or ethnicity can become our primary identity and reason for existence. During severe trials and tests we need to be centered on God and be hidden and lost in God for our name and identity if we are going to progress instead of regress. (See Colossians 3:3.)

Temptation 2: Turn these stones into bread = performance

The enemy tries to get us into a performance trap in which we must do good works to prove to ourselves and to God that we deserve salvation and grace, or we attempt to accomplish great things for God to prove to ourselves and God that we have intrinsic value. The problem with this is that we all fall short of the glory of God. This mentality is a slippery slope that leads to a place where we are never fully satisfied. We can never earn God's love by what we accomplish. There will always be a lot of things left undone, not done the right way, or done the wrong way because we are fallible, sinful humans. When we are caught in a performance trap, we find ourselves working harder and harder to please God even though we feel worse and worse about ourselves. Some even feel worse about themselves when praying and reading the Bible more and more hours because they are attempting to earn God's love by works.

Since we are not saved by works, the only way we can please God is to be in Christ, who has become our wisdom, redemption, and righteousness (Eph. 2:8–9; 1 Cor. 1:30).

Temptation 3: Jump off the roof because God will protect you = presumption

Often when we are in the wilderness we do not hear God's voice clearly because of anxiety and frustration. To compensate for how we feel, we begin to do our own activities to try to make something happen for God. Instead, we need to learn the difference between faith and presumption. Presumption is when we make our own plans, and then after they are in motion, we ask God to bless them. This is because there is a root of pride and there is independence from God. Psalm 19:13 includes a prayer that asks God to keep us from presumptuous sins: "Also keep back Your servant from presumptuous sins; let them not rule over me; then I will be blameless, and I shall be acquitted of great transgression."

Many Christians have made many important decisions without getting proper counsel and without waiting upon the Lord in order to know His will. Some have moved out of state, left their jobs for other jobs, or even married quickly without advice or marriage counseling. They then expect the church and God to bless their decisions, and when God doesn't bless them, they get angry at God and backslide (Prov. 19:3).

When we fail to consistently submit our hearts to God's will and do not regularly pour over God's Word, we will invariably live in presumption because we are outside of His revealed will.

Temptation 4: Bow down to me, and I will give you the kingdom = the sin of expecting power without process and pain

Satan offered Jesus all the kingdoms of the world in an instant because he knew that Jesus' ultimate goal was that all the kingdoms and kings of the earth would come to Him and bow down to Him in worship. (See Daniel 7:13–14.) Jesus' temptation was that He would receive in an instant what would have taken more than three years and much pain to accomplish. God never bypasses the process and the pain that comes with the process because what is done in you is often more important than what is done through you!

God always determines that power and purpose are to be surrounded by problems and pain so that when we have the power, we will not want the glory that comes with the power! When something comes too easily, or if something seems too good to be true, then it probably isn't true or isn't good for you! Many of us want quick fixes and instant answers to our situations, but that is only like experiencing a sugar high, which stimulates you quickly for a short time, but soon you are tired and you need another sugar fix. Ultimately it ruins you physically. Consequently if you are in the wilderness, take heed of the four main tests God will allow you to experience. After Jesus passed these tests, He was ready to walk into His destiny and purpose. If He would have failed one of these tests, He would have been unfit for ministry and would not have been able to redeem us.

During challenging seasons in life we need to imitate Christ's responses when He was tested so that we will be able to pass through the wilderness and come into our promised land. Seeking to become conformed to the image of Jesus means developing the attitude and wisdom of Jesus so that more potential can be unleashed. To become a disciple of Jesus, we must allow Him to process us so that we can become fishers of men and His ambassadors to everyone we come in contact with. As we willingly walk through our wilderness experiences, asking God to strengthen us and further equip us rather than rescue us, we move closer and closer to unleashing our full potential. "Therefore, we are ambassadors for Christ, God making his appeal through us. We implore you on behalf of Christ, be reconciled to God" (2 Cor. 5:20).

Chapter 3

Going to Jerusalem

WHEN I FIRST started writing this book, I realized how countercultural it was in regard to the typical worldview of most American men. Although this book is not only for men, as a man I relate more to what men struggle with, hence this introductory focus. Consequently men in particular (I think ladies may not struggle with the same cultural challenges because they are wired differently) will find the principles in this book to be both challenging to their mindset and revolutionary in regard to their life focus and function. The reason for saying this is because many men I come across are depressed and have an inordinate desire to be fulfilled in sports by vicariously living their lives through other men they set up as heroes. This is because in sports there are clear winners and losers, thus satisfying a man's desire to conquer through mastering a skill. Also, because they feel purposeless, men need to live their lives through other men or through a team they can identify with, attempting to fill the void in their hearts.

Part of the reason we men struggle is because of the American cultural way we view manhood, which is based on an individualistic concept of destiny that we have embraced from the rugged individualism we have inherited from the likes of Thomas Jefferson and others. Also influential is the individualistic search for the perfect man or superman (e.g., Greek mythological heroes such as Atlas) that conquers the world for good, a concept we have embraced in this country and reflected in our movie heroes, such as Superman, Batman, Daredevil, Black Panther, Spider-Man, and others. This individualistic search for the perfect man or superman comes from Greek culture's influence on Western culture. Adultery is another symptom of a man's boredom with himself that comes from not having an overarching purpose that will guide his every decision.

In today's culture there is an emphasis on one's nationality, with ethnic parades and ethnic academic studies, mainly because one's culture becomes the replacement for the lack of an overarching purpose that transcends this physical life. One obvious symptom of this lack of overarching purpose is the prevalence of adultery that has its roots in man's boredom with himself. In my perspective I am first a Christian and second an American (or Italian or Hispanic, etc.). For us to understand how to biblically fulfill our purpose, we need to "go to Jerusalem," which means to desire God above all else, even life itself. And we need to read the Bible with the Hebraic mindset rather than interpret the world through "Athens" (the center of Greek culture two thousand years ago and the center of apologetics with third-century Christian philosophers such as Clement and Origen, who greatly influenced the church with a Greek view of the world).

Traits of the Jesus Principles

As the thesis of this book, we need to understand the principles Jesus used to release greatness in humanity so that we can go from being ordinary to extraordinary people. Truly the Jesus principles involve countercultural traits we need to embrace if we are to fulfill our destiny. Let's examine each of these four traits individually.

Be a team player.

Many men want their individual gifts to shine. However, when it comes to fulfilling destiny, we have to be more like a basketball point guard, such as Steve Nash of the old Phoenix Suns or Magic Johnson of the old Los Angeles Lakers, than a professional golfer, such as Tiger Woods. Golf, unlike life, is a one-person sport. To be successful, men need to learn to leverage their lives by surrounding themselves with people who have strengths they don't have in order to compensate for their weaknesses.

No one has all the gifts, wisdom, power, abilities, and experience necessary to succeed in this life. God has stacked the deck in our lives a certain way so that we are forced to depend on the "dream team" He has already given us if we will just open our eyes of faith and find those team members. First Corinthians 12:8 teaches that God has given some a "word" of wisdom, another a "word" of knowledge because as individuals all we have are fragments. It is the collective gifts and talents of a team that seeks God, while comparing notes and hearing and doing what the Spirit is saying, that will be able to enable individual destinies.

It is not an accident that Jesus chose twelve men, not just one or two, to be His apostles. It is also not an accident that these twelve had to learn to walk together, to grow together, to challenge and lift each other up as a team in order to follow Jesus. Like with team sports, it is through the grid of relational dynamics that we learn to mature in our gifting and become extraordinary people. As men, we need to walk in corporate destiny in order to fulfill our individual destiny.

In the Bible only those who connect to a local church or some corporate body can actually fulfill their destiny, because the Bible was written to a nation (Old Testament) and to the city churches (New Testament). In the Jewish mindset it was unthinkable to be outside the camp and still walk in God's promises. In Numbers 12:14 we see how being outside the camp was a sign of a curse. Yet there are approximately forty million American Christians attempting to serve God without connecting to a local church! This would be as foolish as someone thinking he or she could go to Iraq and defeat terrorists alone. Biblical passages such as James 4:7 and Ephesians 6:10–18 were admonitions for the local church to resist the devil, not just for individuals. Men must get to a place where they lay their extreme individualism aside in order to corporately maximize their purpose in life.

Build and experience covenant relationships.

Many American and Western men have a hard time showing their emotions or admitting when they have a weakness. It is almost unmanly to cry or admit that you cannot do something!

In regard to showing emotions, the greatest man who ever lived, Jesus Christ, was a person totally in touch with His emotions. In the Gospel of John 11:35, Jesus openly and profusely wept, in Mark 1:41 He was moved with compassion, in Mark 3:5 He looked at people with anger, in Luke 10:21 He was filled with joy, and in John 12:27 and Matthew 26:38 He spoke about His soul (emotions) being exceedingly sorrowful.

Men need to learn that being in touch with and expressing their emotions actually makes them more capable as men instead of making them less manly. Wise men know they need accountable relationships in which they can receive counsel and encouragement to continue moving forward. That is why it is important for men to build and experience covenant relationships with other men who are willing and able to be vulnerable with one another. Such relationships are a primary key that enables a man to persevere in his purpose. It was a liberating thing when I came to Christ and He began to show me that He has assigned others to me that would both minister to me and aid me when I am weak. I have noticed that those who isolate themselves when they begin to struggle are no longer in the faith that I have kept by His grace since 1978.

Honor spiritual fathers.

The Bible teaches us to rise in the presence of the aged (Lev. 19:32). In the East they tend to honor older people, but in American culture the marketing for most products and television shows is for folks between the ages of eighteen and thirty-five (except for pharmaceutical ads) because in this nation we glorify three things: sex, power, and glamour! For too long we have been encouraging older men to quit working and retire to Florida to spend the rest of their lives playing golf and watching television. This mindset is even imbedded in city and federal jobs in some places. I was recently with a man who was forced to retire from the New York Police Department just because he reached the age of sixty-two, even though he was healthy and on the force for more than thirty-five years and had a wealth of experience to share with the younger men and women in blue.

There is no such thing as retirement in the Bible. Biblically speaking, the older you get, the more of God you understand and the more experience you have to share with others. God showed me years ago that my greatest ministry is actually going to start when I turn sixty-five. I am looking forward to growing older because I understand that the greatest years of my life in regard to the impact I will have on this world lie ahead of me, not behind me. American men need to surround themselves with older men they can respect and honor so they can build upon their shoulders and do even better instead of disdaining them and setting them aside. Truly all men need older, mature, Christlike mentors in their lives to release them to their destiny. Although Jesus was only thirty years old when He began ministering (Luke 3:23), He actually existed before Abraham (John 8:58), and gave input to His twelve as the Ancient of Days (Dan. 7:9–10; Rev. 1:13–15). It was only after His disciples walked with Him for several years that He ascended into heaven and entrusted them with building His church.

Live with a sense of purpose.

Men who have no purpose in life tend to indulge themselves with the lusts of the flesh and are the most miserable of all people. I have found my greatest joy is when I finish work the Lord has given me for a particular task. Then, when I relax, I am filled with a euphoric spiritual feeling that is greater than any physical pleasure (John 17:4)! All men were born with an innate desire to nurture and protect their families, to empower the helpless, and to die for a cause greater than themselves. Those who are missing even one of these elements in their lives will walk around depressed due to feeling a lack of inner fulfillment or will be addicted to some pleasure because they are attempting to medicate themselves to drown out the powerful voice of God calling them to fulfill their vocation in life.

The Importance of Patience

One of the most important attributes needed to unleash potential is patience. As we go through God's building process, we must be patient with ourselves and those we are called to mentor or lead. We read in Numbers 14:20–38 that a whole generation of the children of Israel failed to reach their potential and enter the Promised Land because they were filled with unbelief and gave in to grumbling and complaining against the Lord. They became impatient with God's process and lost their inheritance.

Instead of destroying the whole nation for their sin and unbelief, God patiently waited until the next generation was ready to take the Promised Land. This teaches us that God will not promote us unless we pass the tests of faith and patience while in our wilderness experiences. It also reminds us that God's purposes cannot be thwarted even by our impatience. If we are unwilling to do what it takes to accomplish God's plans, they will be fulfilled through the lives of the next generation.

When Jesus chose His future leaders, He knew it was going to take several years of work to get them to the place where they would be able to walk in their divine purpose. He had to exercise great patience with those He chose to follow Him. Peter, for example, was a compulsive, rough fisherman given to emotional outbursts. John the beloved, who wrote the great passages on love in 1 John 3 and 4, initially had such a bad temper that Jesus named him and his brother James the sons of thunder!

For three years the disciples witnessed firsthand the powerful potential available to those who followed the Master's example. When Jesus sent them out two by two to implement the lessons they had learned at His feet, they returned with great joy, announcing that even the demons submitted to them when they exercised their authority in His name. Yet as Jesus approached the time of His arrest and crucifixion, He found all His disciples sleeping rather than praying. A member of His inner circle, Judas, betrayed Him to His enemies and later hung himself because of guilt. The other disciples left Him and fled in fear when He was arrested. Peter, the rock on whom Jesus was to build His church, even denied that he knew Jesus. Truly it takes a lot of patience when helping others realize and unleash potential! It is also true that there is no more significant job we are called to do than to be committed to another person's success and aid the person in his or her quest to walk in the person's purpose. Remember also that when we fail, we need patience with ourselves as well. Proverbs 24:16 says "though the righteous fall seven times, they rise again" (NIV).

Because the church I helped pioneer was at one time in a low-income community, we had to nurture indigenous servant leaders instead of hiring established ministers. This turned out to be a great blessing to me personally because it has forced me to focus on maturing leaders instead of importing people who serve for pay and don't share my vision or have a heart of loyalty for our church and mission. I have had to learn to solve leadership challenges by first checking out those we already had with us. Most of the time the people resources we need for any given situation are already available to us right in our midst. I just had to learn how to unleash potential.

As difficult as it is at times to help people mature, I find that the teacher learns as much as or more than the student. In the process of aiding people in their challenges, I found myself stretched and forced to practice what I have been preaching to others. There are obstacles common to all of us in the process of growing and learning. As I lead others, I have to continually overcome those obstacles in myself in order to keep the level of my own abilities high enough to empower others to reach their "higher lid" potential. If I am going to attract those with the potential for high-impact influence, then I have to stay ahead of the game and continue to grow and unleash my own potential. Many pastors and organizational leaders lose their most productive people because they have personally stopped growing. When those under them eventually surpass them and find they can no longer grow, they will look elsewhere for opportunities to develop and unleash more of their own potential.

If I am called to help a person who has put limitations on himself because of low self-esteem and past negative experiences, I have to make sure I am not limiting myself because of my past. If the person I am mentoring is not emotionally mature and doesn't have the discipline and focus that it takes to sustain long-term personal growth, I need to be emotionally mature enough to walk in love and not overreact to his or her flakiness or lack of discipline. Whenever we invest our time in other people, we should find ourselves growing in the process. Proverbs 11:25 says the "one who waters will himself be watered."

Five Stages of Spiritual Development

As I reflect on my own journey, as well as observing the lives of many other believers, I have come to the conclusion that there are at least five major stages of spiritual development. I base this on almost four decades of church and marketplace ministry, which includes serving as a lead pastor since 1984. These five stages are important for us to understand so that we do not become confused when we transition from one stage to the next. However, there are some who stunt their own development through disobedience to their calling. This results in not experiencing anything past the second stage. Additionally, there is no set time for each stage, and since I am using a broad stroke, each stage may overlap other stages at times. That being said, there is truth in these general observations. My objective is to encourage believers to press through to all five stages, no matter how difficult.

1. The honeymoon stage

This is the stage when we are excited about our newly found salvation. Jesus told us to rejoice because our names are written in the Book of Life (Luke 10:17–20). In this stage we are not thinking about our calling; we are just excited about finding this new life in Christ. Nothing else matters except Jesus! It's sort of like when you first fall in love with that special someone, and the goose bumps and romantic feelings are so amazing you cannot picture it ever leaving you! However, as good as this stage is, God prods us along into the next stage, which is experience.

2. The experiential stage

This is the stage when we begin to figure out how to walk with God, and where we begin to learn how to process our faith during the challenges and minutia of everyday life. It is here in the experiential stage that we learn how to apply our faith to our personal lives, families, spheres of influence, and responsibilities. This is also the stage in which we learn how to respond and repent in the midst of our own shortcomings and sins. In this stage we also begin to learn how to "work out [our] own salvation with fear and trembling" (Phil. 2:12). Generally this is the stage that uses tests and trials to reveal our heart, motives, and level of commitment to Christ. This is the stage Jesus taught in the parable of the sower and the seed that illustrates how people fall away from Him because they have no strong roots due to persecution and a lack of understanding the Word of God (Mark 4).

3. The discovery stage

This is the stage in which we first become aware that we have a purpose and calling in Christ. It is an exciting stage, as we realize that we were not just saved to go to heaven but to walk in a divine purpose. This is when we first realize that God has called us to have a major impact in our spheres of influence, whether with a few or with many. Here in the discovery stage the Spirit of God will challenge us to be responsible as His stewards to manifest His kingdom on earth as it is in heaven (Luke 11:2–4).

4. The passion-to-walk-in-purpose-and-identity stage

After we discover the fact that we have a purpose, we almost become obsessed with identifying that purpose through analyzing our natural gifts, abilities, and personality, as well as through what we sense God is calling us to do. This is the stage in which we learn to walk a purpose-driven life and begin investing our time in learning and growing in our capacity as Christ followers. This is also the stage in which we begin to sift our time commitments and relationships so that we can streamline our focus and hit the mark of our divine calling. Although this is an exciting stage, it is not the most important one. Up until recently I thought this particular stage was the most rewarding and highest of all stages; however, the next stage is by far the most important one.

5. The unison stage

This fifth stage is when we experience such oneness with Christ that we no longer obsess over our purpose or identity because we have lost our functional life in Him (Gal. 2:19–21). Jesus' prayer to the Father was that His followers would be "one" with the Father and with Him (John 17:20–24). Although there is a positional and legal element to oneness that has nothing to do with us, my experience has shown me that there is also an existential and experiential oneness. Some may even label this stage mystical. I have referred to this stage as "unison" because it describes the reality of losing one's self in Him to the point where our desires, plans, and passions emanate out of His heart

31

and will. In this stage you are walking in freedom and an almost unbroken fellowship with Him while being even more acutely aware of your own shortcomings and unholy motivations and desires. In this stage not only do you treasure your times worshipping and adoring God, but you begin to learn to delight in doing His will no matter how painful and joyless it may seem at time (Heb. 12:1–2).

In the unison stage we learn that the highest expression of loving God is not just enjoying the person and presence of God but in putting our flesh on the cross and obeying Him without complaining and remorse (Luke 22:42; Rom. 6:6–9). In this stage we live to express Christ alone, and anything else, including our individual purpose, becomes boring and unappealing compared with His splendor and majesty!

I discovered the unison stage initially out of concern that I had become bored with thinking about my purpose and identity. It wasn't that I was disinterested in my calling anymore; on the contrary, I am even more passionate now than ever about serving Christ! It was that I found myself so consumed, enamored, and identified with Jesus that I intuitively knew that my calling would unfold organically as I continued to walk in His steps. I have discovered that Christ is all (Col. 1:16–19)!

In reflection I also discovered that when we are obsessed or passionate about our divine purpose, it can still be about us and not Him. Moreover, being passionate about our purpose is still showing more spiritual development than the first three stages, but it is not the highest level of faith and practice. Scripture informs us that the apostle Paul said that the high calling of God was to know Christ Jesus to the point that he even counted as dung all things, that he may win Christ (Phil. 3:4–11).

The temptation here, of course, is to think you are already in the fifth stage because your spirit leaps when you read about it and your rational mind agrees with the concept. However, it takes years of brokenness, pouring over scripture, and emotional and spiritual growth before you begin to grasp this degree of unison. Of course nobody will fully arrive at the unison stage, because plumbing the depths of the knowledge and love of God continues throughout eternity. All I am saying is, I am now aware of and experiencing this stage because I am truly unimpressed and bored with all notions of self-significance, accomplishments, and anything less than conforming to His image (Rom. 8:29–30).

In conclusion, my prayer is that the truths regarding the process of maturity in Christ will encourage all of us to continue to press on to know the Lord (Hos. 6:3) and "that according to the riches of his glory he may grant you to be strengthened with power through his Spirit in your inner being, so that Christ may dwell in your hearts through faith—that you, being rooted and grounded in love, may have strength to comprehend with all the saints what is the breadth and length and height and depth, and to know the love of Christ that surpasses knowledge, that you may be filled with all the fullness of God" (Eph. 3:16–20).

Chapter 4

Understanding Affirmation

IT HAS BEEN my observation that most of the feedback we get daily is negative. Whether it is the horrible reports we are exposed to in the media or the interactions we have with family, coworkers, and bosses, the overwhelming majority of information we receive is negative either about someone else or about ourselves. Author and personal growth expert Shad Helmstetter said, "As much as 77 percent or more of everything that is recorded and stored in our subconscious minds is counterproductive and works against us—in short, that for the most part, we are wired *not* to succeed!"[1] So how do we combat negative thinking? We combat negative thinking through affirmation. Affirmation helps neutralize negativity. I have heard it stated that it takes thirty words of affirmation to neutralize one negative hit to a person's self-worth. The Bible speaks plainly about the power of words. "From the fruit of a man's mouth his stomach is satisfied; he is satisfied by the yield of his lips. Death and life are in the power of the tongue, and those who love it will eat its fruits" (Prov. 18:20–21).

Leaders have the ability to motivate people to make a long-term commitment (to a cause) based on communicating a compelling vision. Jesus demonstrated this beautifully for us. Hence, vision enables people to picture a better future that they, themselves, own and create by the proper allocation and utilization of their gifts and talents.

When Kristian first came into our church, the only thing he saw and felt was the forgiveness of God and joy of salvation. He wasn't thinking of anything but the fact that he was on his way to heaven. But when I saw him, not only did I see a new believer; I also sensed his calling to be a preacher of the gospel and a leader of others. He seemed so gifted in those areas and had a definite desire to help others. As a pastor one of the most important jobs I have is to perceive and declare people's future even if they themselves can't see it because of spiritual ignorance or self-limitations. I immediately took Kristian into one of my mentoring groups, began to spend a lot of time with him, and had him traveling with me when I went to minister in other churches. Although he didn't understand what was going on, I was mentoring him and preparing him for his future; first as a man and second as a minister of the gospel.

Not long after his conversion, I began declaring to Kristian what I saw in his future so that he would begin to believe it and have something to work toward in his life.

Though the words I spoke to him were not words anybody else had spoken to him, he received what I said because I was merely echoing what God had already embedded within his soul. As I told him about his unique calling and affirmed him in his gifts and talents, he began to embrace the vision of who he could become. As this vision became real to him, it began to release his potential. He started sharing the gospel on the street and winning people to Christ. Within a year he became a confident and effective small-group leader, helping others grow and release their potential. His incredible journey from a typical fatherless teenager with no purpose in life to a significant leader started with words of affirmation and faith that gave him a vision of his future.

When Jesus first met Simon Peter, James, and John, they were partnering together in a fishing business, believing their only purpose in life was to work hard all day making a living for their families. In order for Jesus to unleash their higher calling, which was to become fishers of men for the kingdom of God, He couldn't just preach at them. He had to get into their world by getting into their boat with them. Jesus saw the innermost thoughts of people and what they were to be in the future when their potential was unleashed. After he demonstrated that He was Lord of the animal kingdom and able to catch more fish in one moment than they would be able to all night, more than adequately providing for them and their families, they were ready to listen to what He had to say. Jesus could now speak vision to them, and as a result they readily gave up their business to follow and learn from Him.

But this was only the beginning of the process Jesus would use to unleash the human potential in His disciples. Jesus had to keep reminding them of their calling, correcting them, affirming them, and guiding them on the correct path. He had to patiently teach and model for them how to be poor in spirit and mourn the sins of others. They had to learn how to be gentle, merciful peacemakers who could endure persecution for righteousness' sake. Jesus continuously demonstrated for them how to live a life of obedience to God's Word so that they could bring light to a darkened world and salt to those who needed physical, emotional, and spiritual healing. Jesus spoke into their lives, telling them that eventually they would do even greater works than He did.

Balancing Correction With Affirmation

One of the key ingredients Jesus used in unleashing potential in His disciples was balancing correction with affirmation. Even Jesus Himself didn't begin His ministry until He was affirmed by His Father. We read in the Gospel of Matthew how the Father said, "and behold, a voice from heaven said, 'This is my beloved Son, with whom I am well pleased'" (3:17). This affirmation from the Father prepared Jesus to face Satan's temptation and enter full-time ministry. One of the reasons many fail in their lives and calling is that they have not received the affirmation from their mentors that prepares them for the spiritual warfare and temptation that is sure to come. Without adequate affirmation, low self-esteem and lack of confidence can cause many to falter and quit when times get tough. Remembering words of affirmation and knowing that our mentors are in our corner gives us the courage we need to continue through our life's experiences in spite of all the temptations and trials we face along the way.

Jesus practiced this with His disciples. For example, when He saw Nathaniel come to Him, Jesus told him that he was an Israelite who had no guile (John 1:47). Likewise, Jesus called Simon the "rock" upon which He would build His church (Matt. 16:18–19) in spite of the fact that Simon was impetuous and was going to betray Jesus in the near future! Jesus used words to help shape, motivate, and form His followers, which released them to their purpose through the power of affirmation.

There are also numerous examples of how Jesus used the power of affirming words (and at times the power of a physical touch) to bring healing to an individual:

- Jesus cast many evil influences of demons out with a word (Matt. 8:16).

- Jesus healed a leper with both an affirming word and a personal touch (Mark 1:40–45; Luke 5:12–16).

- Jesus spoke a word and told a blind beggar that he could receive His sight (Mark 10:46–52).

- Jesus spoke a word and cast out a spirit of weakness from a woman hunched over for eighteen years (Luke 13:11–13).

- Jesus changed the life of the woman at the well by offering her living water (John 4:7–30).

- Jesus told a sick man with a victim spirit to rise up, pick up his bed, and walk (John 5:1–9).

I have personally felt the impact of the power of words spoken over my life by mentors and overseers. As a young man maturing in my ministry calling, I remember how the words of my spiritual father had the power to bring great joy into my life or great confusion and depression.

One way I was able to intuit who my spiritual father was, was when I cared about what a particular overseer thought of me. That was a sign to me that God connected us together in a father-son relationship. This is because I knew that part of the role of a father is to give much needed affirmation, even as the Lord Jesus needed the affirmation of His Father before He ministered (Luke 3).

I remember one time I spent hours driving to spend time with my original overseer, who had moved on from the pastorate in which he served. When I got there, his plans changed, and he handed me money so I could buy myself some dinner. Although he meant well, he did not understand how his lack of attention to me crushed me emotionally. At that point I knew that I was not a priority to him anymore (because of his move out of state), and I began to pray about finding another overseer who would also serve as a spiritual father to me. By God's providence I was eventually connected to my current overseer, John Kelly, who has been an amazing spiritual dad to me since 1989. God has used him tremendously to help shape and form me through his words, strategic abilities, and powerful ministry. I would not be where I am today apart from his role in my life as a spiritual father!

The power of affirming words and actions has also been integrated biologically by God to affect the whole person even according to science. Take for instance the strategic way God designed the human brain, integrating all its parts. Biologically speaking, God created our brains to have an intellectual part, the cerebral cortex, and an emotional part, the limbic brain (shaped sort of like a hot dog running from our foreheads to the backs of our heads underneath the gray matter we are so used to seeing when we see pictures of the brain). According to the Centre for Neuro Skills, "The brain stem plays a vital role in basic attention, arousal, and consciousness. All information to and from our body passes through the brain stem on the way to or from the brain."[2]

There are millions of connections between the three parts of our brains. Some people are too emotional and don't use their intellectual brains, doing whatever their emotional impulses lead them to do. Others are too intellectual and not in touch with feelings, causing all sorts of unconscious emotional and spiritual problems without even being aware of the emotional component to them.

Jesus used all of His brain and wants us to do the same.

He set a perfect example, not only by having supernatural intelligence but also by demonstrating for us His emotional side, including weeping, grieving, getting angry, and loving His dear family and friends. The Bible teaches us that if we see loved ones weeping, we should not go up to them and encourage them to quit weeping, but rather we should give them a hug and "weep with those who weep" (Rom. 12:15). Jesus used His sensitivity to the human condition to release words and touch to affect the brain function of other people, thus resulting in not just physical but also emotional healing. He was a master at bringing about an internal rewiring and recalibration to each person who encountered Him in faith.

Even science teaches us that words have the power to positively alter the brain, which in turn will alter the whole body.

In my own research I have found that words have the power to alter the genes that regulate our emotional and physical stress. Positive words engage motivational components of our brains, which catalyzes action. Furthermore, cognitive reasoning is increased and our frontal lobes strengthened when we say and hear positive words. Contrawise, negative words inhibit the neurochemicals that manage stress. They actually release stress-producing hormones into our neurological and biological systems. Consequently the fear that is released by negative words impedes our ability to reason by limiting the capacity of our frontal lobes. (For more detail on this topic, read

Words Can Change Your Brain by Dr. Andrew Newberg and Mark Robert Waldman.)

In summary, the key to changing all other areas of our brains is to concentrate on positive things. Even the section of the brain called the thalamus, which affects the way we perceive reality, can be altered by our words.

The Sandwich Approach

We know, of course, that correction is also often needed as we walk this path toward unleashing potential. I have heard it said that for every single correction we give to our children, we need to give them ten words of affirmation and encouragement! We also need to do this with those we are mentoring as they move toward fulfilling their destiny. An easy way to remember this is to use the "sandwich approach" to balance affirmation and correction. The "sandwich approach" is this: The pieces of bread on the outside of the sandwich are metaphors for starting and ending your conversation with praise or some form of positive affirmation. The meat in the middle of the sandwich is the correction. As simple or silly as this may sound, it is actually quite effective because it is easy to remember and, if followed, enables us to keep a proper perspective when there is a need for constructive correction. Unleashing a person's potential is much more effective when we balance our focus on the positive traits of a person and not just the negative actions we are helping them to overcome.

Along with the sandwich approach to correction, we need to practice a habit of consistent review. When His disciples returned after He sent them out to preach and minister, Jesus took them aside privately for review and correction (Luke 9:1–27). Proverbs 27:6 teaches us that "faithful are the wounds of a friend, but deceitful are the kisses of an enemy" (NASB). This means that there has to be room for correction in every true relationship; otherwise it is superficial and phony. If I truly love a person and want to help the person fulfill his or her potential, I have to be honest and bring correction when necessary, just as Jesus did.

Proverbs 9:8 declares that if you rebuke or correct a wise man, he will love you for it. But if you rebuke a fool, he will hate you for it, so don't waste your time with him. If you carefully speak the truth in love, giving accurate but polite and respectful rebukes to those you are mentoring, and use the sandwich approach to balance affirmation with correction, you will have good results. However, if the person you are mentoring thinks he is perfect and refuses to accept correction, quit mentoring him and spend your time with someone teachable.

Remember that God gives us choices. Three things determine how much potential we will unleash: our genes, our environment (especially in the growing-up years), and our choices. Bad genes can usually be overcome with proper diet and sometimes medication. A bad childhood environment can be healed with good Christian counseling and good mentoring. Yet the greatest factor in our lives is the choices we make. I know people who inherited great genes, had awesome parents, and attended a healthy church, and still ended up in horrible places emotionally and spiritually because of the poor choices they made along the way.

As parents we all make mistakes, but when our kids grow up, we still have to turn them over to God and not blame ourselves for the ultimate choices they make. The same applies to those we mentor. Jesus offered His unconditional love, taught sound principles, and led an exemplary life before all His disciples. Yet Judas made poor choices and took his own life rather than unleash his true potential. The children of Israel failed to obey the Word of the Lord and enter their Promised Land because they saw themselves as grasshoppers and their opponents as giants. Their low self-esteem fed into their unbelief and destroyed their destiny! In Kristian's life the words I spoke to him and the scriptures he read gradually erased the picture he had of himself. His openness to grow enabled the Spirit of God to paint a completely new picture of him on the canvas of his heart! God wants to do the same for all of us.

Chapter 5

Loving and Being Loved

HUMANS ARE THE only living species on planet Earth that are said to be made in the image and likeness of God; therefore, we have almost unlimited potential (Gen. 1:26)! Romans 8:29 says that God's purpose for us is to become conformed to the image of Christ. First John 4:17 teaches us that as Jesus is, so are believers to be in this world. This does not mean that God's purpose for us is to wear a robe, grow a beard, have a public ministry, and die on a cross. Jesus epitomized God's love for us by laying aside all that it meant to be God to come to the earth as a man. His unselfish, sacrificial love was displayed for all to see as He died a tortuous death on the cross so mankind could be forgiven for those things we do in life that hurt others or ourselves.

Conforming to the image of Jesus means we have the

opportunity to become better at loving and accepting love from others. The more we love, develop an others-focused attitude, and apply the wisdom of Jesus, the more our human potential is unleashed. Like Jesus, we are called to do great and loving things now, while we are alive in this world.

I have found that most people do not care about my education, my titles, or the friendships I have with celebrities and powerful people. The truth is, people don't care how much you know. They only want to know how much you care. If I am to help others unleash their human potential, I have to be much more than a professional member of the clergy or a leadership consultant. I have to be a mentor, in some cases a coach, and in some more exceptional cases a spiritual or surrogate father. Sometimes an individual's human potential is stunted until I step in and help heal the wounds caused by the absence or abandonment of an earthly parent or guardian.

In the New Covenant, God reveals Himself to us in a personal way, not as "the great Apostle" or "the general" but as our "heavenly Father." It was our heavenly Father who created us and assigned each of us the gifts and abilities that determine our potential. Then He gave each of us an earthly father to help us unleash that potential. Often we are given both a natural father and a spiritual father to guide us through the process necessary for achieving our full potential. Even though I have been consecrated a bishop and have earned a doctorate, the most important title I have is when the men and women in the church call me "Dad" or "Pop." Being a spiritual parent is possibly the highest calling of any potential mentor, coach, or leader because in that function we are truly exemplifying God's love.

This is especially important in our present fatherless society, in which many young men have come into our churches with "an orphan spirit" because of being abandoned by their natural fathers. God can use spiritual fathers as surrogate dads to help heal their wounds of rejection and open a door for the love of Father God to heal their wounds and restore them to a healthy place emotionally.

Jesus told us God has called each and every one of us to continue His work here on the earth. He promises us that God has equipped us not only to do what He did but also to accomplish even greater things (John 14:12). Unleashing your human potential means fulfilling the Great Commission and exemplifying the Great Commandment (Matt. 28:19; 22:37–40).

The Dance of Love

Fulfilling the Great Commission and exemplifying the great commandment can only be accomplished by serving God and your fellow man, living a life of balance to protect your sanity, and leaving this world a little better place than it would have been if you had never been born. Most people in this world waste their lives in a silly rat race. All of us, to some extent or another, go through life feeling like a "nobody" while trying to prove to the world that we are a "somebody." How shallow life would be if we served no greater purpose than to merely exist until our time on earth is completed. Unleashing your human potential begins with dedicating your life to serving, laughing, and crying with those you love.

Experience and research have convinced me that the only people in the world who have true happiness and meaning are people who develop the gift of loving and being loved. Since there are high suicide rates even among the wealthiest, thinking financial success is the key to becoming extraordinary and unleashing your true potential could be the worst mistake you ever make. I wish financial success for all of you, as long as you keep it in perspective. Loving and being loved by God and using your gifts and talents to serve God and others and thereby fulfilling the great commandment are a thousand times more important than your net worth.

I know plenty of wealthy people who use their time and money to serve God and help humankind and are quite happy. The Bible tells of Abraham and Job, who remained godly men even though they were the wealthiest men on earth at that time. In the Book of Ecclesiastes, King Solomon encourages wealthy people to enjoy their wealth but not to live for it. Yet a higher percentage of wealthy people have made the mistake of living in pursuit of fool's gold rather than the real thing, and they suffer from great loneliness and meaninglessness at the end of their lives. True gold comes from understanding the great commandment and using it to dance with the world, spreading the love of God around.

The Great Commission, in Matthew 28:19–20, which encourages us to go into all the world to spread the gospel of God's love and redemption (in the passive imperative tense in the original Greek so it is more accurately translated) says, "As you are going about in the world, spread the good news." As we go throughout our area of the world, we are called to be God's love letters to everyone we come into contact with.

The apostle Paul, who wrote most of the New Testament epistles, praised those he had personally discipled in Corinth for the love they showed to the rest of the world through their genuine loving acts and attitudes. In 2 Corinthians 3:2–3 he gave them the highest compliment he could possibly give anyone, describing those disciples as epistles or love letters to the world from Jesus. "Clearly, you are a letter from Christ showing the result of our ministry among you. This 'letter' is written not with pen and ink, but with the Spirit of the living God. It is carved not on tablets of stone, but on human hearts" (NLT). God does not call all of us to become professional, full-time, foreign missionaries, but He does call us all to be full-time representatives of His love.

The Personal Touch

Mark Twain has been quoted as saying, "It's usually not what you eat that gives you indigestion—it's what's eating you!" If we are going to be successful in helping others become extraordinary, then we need to be personally engaged with them and discover the root cause of anything hindering the maximization of purpose. Just placing a person in some kind of official program can never take the place of the personal touch that every individual needs. A recent *New York Times* article stated there is now scientific evidence related to how personal physical touch actually improves the performance and attitude of individuals.[1]

Researchers have said regarding physical contact, "Momentary touches, they say—whether an exuberant high five, a warm hand on the shoulder, or a creepy touch to the arm—can communicate an even wider range of emotion than gestures or expressions, and sometimes do so more quickly and accurately than words....The evidence that such messages can lead to clear, almost immediate changes in how people think and behave is accumulating fast."[2]

That physical touch can even enhance performance in athletic competition is being researched. "To see whether a rich vocabulary of supportive touch is in fact related to performance, scientists at Berkeley recently analyzed interactions in one of the most physically expressive arenas on earth: professional basketball. Michael W. Kraus led a research team that coded every bump, hug and high five in a single game played by each team in the National Basketball Association early last season." The results of the study indicated that "good teams tended to be touchier than bad ones."[3] There really is power in physical touch. Of course physical touch and hugs can also be used sinfully by predators, so be careful whom, when, and where you hug.

A Comprehensive Approach

Some victims of various forms of childhood abuse are full of negative self-talk, an erroneous low opinion of themselves, and a fear of intimacy from the loving people around them. Some have a variety of genetic factors that make them more prone to developing unwanted symptoms such as bipolar disorder, obsessive-compulsive disorder, ADHD, or various types of genetic depressions. Some have genetic factors that cause them to suffer emotional pain and fatigue. Others have nutritional factors contributing to their depression. Poor nutrition affects billions throughout the world, even rich Americans who live on unhealthy foods.

To release human potential, we need to employ a comprehensive approach, looking at any and all factors that may be contributing to the unwanted symptoms that are stifling a person's ability to unleash his or her potential. There are also those who are passive and controlled by others who need to be more assertive and independent. Other people are laden down with loads of repressed anger from various types of abuse and can eventually unleash that anger in unhealthy ways that destroy relationships.

You can verbally affirm people with praises for a job well done, but you can also affirm them with a pat on the back, a warm handshake, and appropriate hugs. When we study the life of Jesus, we see how warm and affectionate He was in touching and being touched by those around Him. I believe one of the most important things Jesus did to unleash the vast potential in His disciples was to be informal and personal with them. At the Last Supper we see John the apostle leaning on Christ's chest, which shows the correlation among love, acceptance, personal touch, and leadership development. Jesus called His closest disciples His friends, not His servants. He was open and real with them and disclosed to them the intimate things the Father spoke to Him in private. Jesus treated His disciples the same way God treated Moses, whom He knew face to face, and Abraham, whom He called His friend. As Jesus hung on the cross, one of the last things He did was choose John to take His place as Mary's son and to take care of her. In a sense Jesus was showing He also viewed John and His disciples as His brothers, not just as members of a religious order.

Taking my cue from Christ, I realized a long time ago that my primary job as a pastor is to develop sons and daughters, not just employees and church members. My personal touch and affirmation of them as part of my spiritual family will motivate them to become all they can be. They will in turn mentor others in the same personal way. Conversely, when mentors and leaders are not real with the people they are training, they show that they are either socially dysfunctional or have a problem with trusting others. Their followers will further perpetuate this dysfunction among those they are training, teaching, and mentoring.

I generally recommend that pastors, mentors, and leaders also have close friends who are peers to mutually encourage them. Often another pastor, mentor, or leader in a similar field is a good person to buddy up to. The only people who have joy and meaning in this life are those who have a few friends they can love and be loved by unconditionally.

Treating people as friends means that you share intimate things with them, you bare your heart and soul to them, you hang out with them, have fun with them, and enjoy their company in the midst of all the work you perform together. This is in contrast to a boss-hireling business arrangement in which people serve in a job. Employees clock in at 9:00 a.m. and leave at 5:00 p.m. on the button, even when there are urgent things left undone, because they care not about the work they do. When leaders treat people as friends, we demonstrate that relationship is the basis of our work together, which engenders a spirit of proprietorship and begins to unleash the potential within others.

Look at what the disciples of Jesus accomplished in a world without cars, planes, phones, and computers after less than three years under His mentorship. Can you imagine the potential that can be released in those we are called to lead and mentor with all that is available in the world today?

Religion or Relationship

One of the most pervasive things in the church world today is a performance-based Christianity that is more religious in nature than relational. This expression of Christianity is prevalent in church cultures that are replete with religious practices but lacking in transparent, genuine relationships. As I read the New Testament, I find that the kingdom of God is not built by ministry but by relationships.

Unfortunately many spiritual leaders only know how to influence people from behind their pulpit and are awkward when informally relating to people in social settings. These leaders are generally aloof and uncomfortable in any setting where they are not in a position of power while ministering to others. Although pulpit ministry is vitally important to help mature people in the faith, a person's potential will be left untapped outside of relationship. Those being mentored need intentional, informal connections with their spiritual leaders.

Young people today are especially craving a genuine, informal, relational Christian experience because they are skeptical of the scandal-plagued, religious, institutional model of church. Although the general term given to describe Christ followers has been "Christians," believers were only called this three times in the New Testament (Acts 11:26; 26:28; 1 Pet. 4:16).

In contrast, Jesus called Himself "the way" (John 14:6), and the early church was described by others as "the Way," as recorded in the Book of Acts (9:2; 19:9, 23; 24:14, 22), and also as "this Life" (Acts 5:20). Consequently if we desire the same results as Jesus and the early church, we need to encourage a culture of faith that is more of a way of life (that is seamlessly integrated organically in our personal life, family, business, and church) rather than the present religious culture that carves out specific times for religious practice and behavior. In other words, in the twenty-first century we need to go backward, to the way of Christ and His apostles, before we will have the trajectory to go forward and experience personal transformation and reach our potential as God designed it. Of course in order to fully understand the New Testament methodology of how Jesus released human potential and made His disciples extraordinary, it is vital for us to understand the cultural and religious background of Jesus and His disciples. With this in mind, it is helpful for us to understand the common discipleship method of the Jewish rabbis during Jesus' day and contrast it with Christ's method so we can gain a greater appreciation of His radical approach based on His claim of lordship.

On the surface there appears to be no essential difference between the discipleship methods of Jesus and that of the rabbis of His time. For example, both Jesus and the rabbis had disciples or students that would personally attach themselves to them. However, a closer examination shows there are fundamental differences between these two approaches. The following shows these contrasts:

- The *talmidim* (rabbis' disciples) chose their own teacher. Jesus chose His own disciples (Luke 9:57–62; John 15:16). Mark 5:18–19 shows how Jesus even rejected some who wanted to follow Him. Jesus was deliberate and intentional about who He would connect Himself to.

- The *talmidim* chose a rabbi based on his knowledge of the Torah (the Old Testament scriptures) because the law was the center of Judaism. A rabbi only had authority commensurate with his knowledge of the Torah; the authority belonged to the Torah, not any individual rabbi. In contrast, Jesus expected

His disciples to renounce everything, not for the sake of the Torah but for His sake alone (Matt. 10:38). In the New Covenant, Jesus is the center of the universe, not the Torah (or the Bible). Read John 5:39–40 and Colossians 1:17. Of course the scriptures bear witness of Christ if read with an unveiled heart. (See 2 Corinthians 3:15–18.)

- In Judaism, being a disciple was only transitional—a means to an end—with the goal of becoming a rabbi. For the disciples of Jesus, discipleship was not a step toward a promising career. Following Jesus was in itself the fulfillment of destiny (Rom. 8:29–30). In other words, there is no graduation or official degree that completes our discipleship process. It is an ongoing process that continues until our last breath in this life and beyond (Phil. 3:7–14; 2 Pet. 3:18).

- Disciples of rabbis were only their students, nothing more. The disciples of Jesus were also His servants who committed themselves to obeying Him and suffering for His sake (Matt. 16:24–25; John 12:26).

- The disciples of rabbis merely passed on their teachings. The disciples of Jesus were called to be with Him (Mark 3:14) and be His witnesses (Acts 1:8).

- The disciples of rabbis were attempting to bring back the former glory of the nation of Israel. The disciples of Jesus were (and still are) the vanguard of the coming kingdom and await the second bodily return of King Jesus.

- For the disciples of rabbinic Judaism, following the letter of the 613 laws and rabbinic interpretations of the Torah was of prime importance. But for Jesus, following the minutia of the ceremonial law was not as important as caring for the human soul (Mark 2:1–12; 3:1–6).

- The Jewish rabbis stressed separation from non-Jews and those that were unclean. Jesus taught that loving our neighbors is equal to loving God irrespective of whether a person is a Jew (Matt. 22:37–40; Luke 10:30–37).[4]

The fact that Jesus always intended His followers to carry on His earthly ministry of releasing greatness in people and advancing His kingdom is clear by referring back to the beginning of the Book of Acts, in which Luke states that his Gospel narrative recorded all Jesus began to say until He was taken into heaven, after which He, by the Holy Spirit, had given orders to His apostles whom He had chosen (Acts 1:1–2). In other words, Jesus passed on His work to His apostles before He ascended into heaven because the Luke narrative is merely a record of what Jesus "began to do." By implication, His work continued through the church, as recorded in the Acts narrative. Hence, if we are truly going to walk in our potential and fulfill our assignment, we need to study the life of Jesus and walk as He walked and invest in others and He invested in them.

Empowering Others

Let me conclude with a slightly paraphrased excerpt based on chapter 11 of my book *An Anthology of Essays on Cutting Edge Leadership*.[5]

The following are ways we can empower others to fulfill their potential:

Empowering people allow others to make mistakes.

Some people are more concerned with getting a job done correctly than with empowering people to learn how to do a job. When all we care about is getting a job done right, we won't truly delegate authority to others to perform a task. This is because we view people merely as an extension of our arms and legs but not our brain. We don't let others think for themselves. Instead, we give the person a task to perform and then constantly correct him or her as the job is being done. On the other hand, empowering people often allow those to whom they assign tasks to make mistakes and then gracefully critique them after each task is completed.

Empowering people don't micromanage.

Micromanaging should only be done if a leader is working with a person who is completely untrained or unskilled at a particular task. This kind of working arrangement should only be temporary because a person should not be assigned a task he or she doesn't have the potential skill to perform. Once the transition to job proficiency is complete, the leader should allow the worker to perform tasks with only macro oversight.

Micromanaging breeds an atmosphere of distrust and tells the person given the task that the leader doesn't really believe in him or her. Habitual micromanagers usually don't have a clue when it comes to empowering others.

Empowering people focus on the positive traits of others.

We all stumble in many ways. All of us usually drop the ball on assignments at least 10 percent of the time, depending on how much extra work we have. In addition to this, there are always going to be mistakes in a certain percentage of the tasks we perform. Also, one person will tend to do a job differently from the next person. Consequently we will always have the opportunity to point out things that a person doesn't do correctly. Thus, we should attempt to focus most on what the person given the task did correctly and the results of the work performed, not on the mistakes. Of course the exception to this is if someone totally messes up a task or doesn't follow the guidelines given.

When we focus on the positive contributions of others,

we impart confidence to them and motivate them to continue to perform at a high level.

Empowering people give constructive criticism, not destructive criticism.

There should be regularly scheduled times after each major task is completed to review the work and assess whether objectives were met. This should be based on the criteria given before the task was attempted so there is an objective way to gauge whether the task was performed with excellence. Regular debriefing allows the person given a task to understand whether he or she is growing in the job and where that person stands in regard to his or her employment.

It is not fair to tell people one year after they start a job that they are not performing well. By this time their job is already in jeopardy, and they haven't even been given a chance to improve because they had no feedback.

Those who desire to work with a spirit of excellence usually welcome consistent, constructive criticism. Of course when leaders put people down, call them names, belittles them, or speak in a condescending manner, they are dispensing criticism that can destroy, not build up, those working under them.

Empowering people give expected guidelines, goals, and outcomes.

Empowering people (leaders, managers in this context) give those working for them general guidelines for jobs and the objectives of tasks, along with the end result they are looking for. This enables the people given the tasks to "run downfield with the ball" creatively without constantly looking over their shoulders, wondering if they are still on the playing field.

Disempowering people merely give people tasks but have amorphous guidelines, goals, and objectives so that no one but the leader really knows if the job is being done right or wrong. When leaders do this, it is a sign that either they, themselves, don't have real objectives for a task or that they are simply trying to exercise psychological control over their workers.

Empowering people help connect other people to their passion, gifts, and calling.

Empowering people always attempt to match people with jobs according to their gifts, passion, and abilities. Disempowering people don't take these things into consideration and often are guilty of attempting to force a square peg into a round hole. Empowering people take pride in being able to help people soar like eagles to the highest heights imaginable, while disempowering people care more about getting tasks accomplished than releasing human potential. Empowering people also are sensitive and lead each person differently according to his or her experience, personality, and temperament.

Empowering people focus on inspiring people as opposed to forcing people to perform.

Empowering people cast vision so as to inspire their followers to perform great things, while disempowering leaders often get things done merely by giving orders and making demands on people. When you inspire people, they perform at a much greater level because they are allowed to make their own decisions to serve and have a greater amount of buy-in, while those merely following orders will do just enough to please the leader and usually don't tap much into their creative juices.

Empowering people engage in dialogue, while disempowering leaders dictate their desires and ideas.

Empowering people attempt to allow a flow of dialogue between themselves and their followers in work-related projects. These leaders understand the importance of receiving regular feedback from their subordinates so they will have a better understanding of how to go about accomplishing tasks. In contrast, people who disempower others don't usually engage in dialogue but merely dictate what and how they want a project done. Folks under this kind of person eventually lose their motivation to think and just robotically follow orders because they know their opinions don't really matter. Dictating leaders usually don't multiply other leaders; they merely retain followers who have allowed their creativity to be capped.

Chapter 6

Unleashing Others' Potential

*J*ESUS CONSTANTLY MODELED leadership (Luke 11:1; John 13:4–15). One of the biggest stumbling blocks for people is when they see their leaders living a double standard. When leaders live with lower standards than the message they preach, it invalidates their teaching and breeds disrespect and animosity toward said leader among his or her followers. We have to have more than just good oratory and rhetoric, and we have to do more than mere sermonizing if we are going to help release potential in people. Truly the most effective tool for releasing potential is mentoring and becoming a role model. Jesus motivated His disciples to achieve greatness by embodying a servant leadership style in which He never asked anyone to do something He didn't first model. The Book of John says:

Jesus, knowing that the Father had given all things into His hands, and that He had come forth from God and was going back to God, got up from supper, and laid aside His garments; and taking a towel, He girded Himself. Then He poured water into the basin, and began to wash the disciples' feet and to wipe them with the towel with which He was girded. So He came to Simon Peter. He said to Him, "Lord, do You wash my feet?" Jesus answered and said to him, "What I do you do not realize now, but you will understand hereafter." Peter said to Him, "Never shall You wash my feet!" Jesus answered him, "If I do not wash you, you have no part with Me." Simon Peter said to Him, "Lord, then wash not only my feet, but also my hands and my head." Jesus said to him, "He who has bathed needs only to wash his feet, but is completely clean; and you are clean, but not all of *you*." For He knew the one who was betraying Him; for this reason He said, "Not all of you are clean." So when He had washed their feet, and taken His garments and reclined at the table again, He said to them, "Do you know what I have done to you? You call Me Teacher and Lord; and you are right, for so I am. If I then, the Lord and the Teacher, washed your feet, you also ought to wash one another's feet. For I gave you an example that you also should do as I did to you. Truly, truly, I say to you, a slave is not greater than his master, nor is one who is sent greater than the one who sent him. If you know these things, you are blessed if you do them."

—JOHN 13:3–17, NASB

By humbling Himself and washing the dirty, smelly, manure, mud-filled feet of His disciples, Jesus was exemplifying the highest form of leadership—that of becoming a servant leader. Servant leaders are very effective because this style of leadership accomplishes three important things. Their service meets the felt needs of the people they lead. It gives servant leaders an opportunity to utilize their gifts and abilities to aid the individuals they are serving. It also results in a high trust level among those they serve because the humility of putting another person's needs first breeds even more trust and gratitude, resulting in a greater openness to receive instruction and impartation for growth. This goes against the top-down approach many leaders try to employ both in the religious world and the marketplace. Sometimes even religious leaders model the opposite of Christ's servant leadership style by being inaccessible to those they are training and by giving the impression that the sheep are there to serve the shepherd instead of the other way around.

This kind of top-down, autocratic, aloof leadership style usually only nurtures followers—people who don't think for themselves and just follow orders. Thus, they are not trained to engage in the kind of critical thinking necessary to develop the kind of problem-solving ability and potential that releases potential. By serving others in the areas we are teaching, we make ourselves accountable to practice something before we attempt to preach about it. I have found that I have the most authority to instruct others in the areas I have already successfully put into practice.

Acts 1:1 says that Jesus did something before He taught it. Most of us have that order in the reverse—we attempt to teach others regarding areas in our lives we, ourselves, have not yet mastered. However, if we are going to learn how to release potential the way Jesus did, we have to "do and teach."

Jesus is the Good Shepherd, who laid down His life for His sheep by serving them by His life and death and resurrection. In the Gospel of John, Jesus Christ says:

> I am the good shepherd; the good shepherd lays down His life for the sheep. He who is a hired hand, and not a shepherd, who is not the owner of the sheep, sees the wolf coming, and leaves the sheep and flees, and the wolf snatches them and scatters them. He flees because he is a hired hand and is not concerned about the sheep.
>
> —JOHN 10:11–13, NASB

The Book of Ezekiel says this about the shepherds who use and abuse the sheep to serve themselves instead of the other way around:

> Son of man, prophesy against the shepherds of Israel. Prophesy and say to those shepherds, "Thus says the Lord GOD, 'Woe, shepherds of Israel who have been feeding themselves! Should not the shepherds feed the flock? You eat the fat and clothe yourselves with the wool, you slaughter the fat sheep without feeding the flock. Those who are sickly you have not strengthened, the diseased you have not healed, the broken you have not bound up, the scattered you

have not brought back, nor have you sought for the
lost; but with force and with severity you have dominated them. They were scattered for lack of a shepherd, and they became food for every beast of the
field and were scattered. My flock wandered through
all the mountains and on every high hill; My flock
was scattered over all the surface of the earth, and
there was no one to search or seek for them.'"

—EZEKIEL 34:2–6, NASB

In regard to this style of leadership, I was personally
impacted in the late 1980s by the servant leadership style of
my overseer, John Kelly, who flew down to spend time with
me and my church leaders even though he was the overseer of a large network of churches and I was only about
thirty years old with a fledgling new inner-city church. On
two separate occasions he spent more than a week with
me, imparting knowledge and strategy and developing a
friendship with me. The effects of his ministry were profound because he was accessible and open and shared his
life with me, not just his professional ministry! He even
spent time taking me to a store in Brooklyn, New York, that
sold men's clothing and taught me how to shop for good
clothes. He went with me to my house and looked at all my
ties, which resulted in my throwing away most of them and
purchasing a whole new wardrobe, both of suits and ties.
His personal involvement with me caused my latent abilities as a strategist to blossom and dramatically aided me in
my citywide influence and even in the administration and
management of Resurrection Church of New York and of a

regional coalition I oversee. He taught me how an organization grows primarily through good administration, not just through anointed preaching, and how a servant leadership approach trumps an aloof, top-down ministry approach in regard to releasing human potential.

Jesus' Leadership Principles

Of course the essence of this book is to learn from the Lord Jesus Christ how to develop and release potential in people. To that end there are at least seven primary principles Jesus utilized to transition people from living an ordinary life to an extraordinary life full of divine purpose and fulfillment. Jesus did not produce disciples and transform lives by mere preaching but by living an exemplary life that those close to Him would emulate. The following are primary ways Jesus empowered and released purpose in Himself and others.

Jesus asked questions.

Instead of just giving the answers to life's questions, Jesus demonstrated that the best way to teach people was to ask them questions. As a matter of fact, He asked over three hundred questions and only gave answers to three of them.[1] When we allow people to answer questions, it reveals how much they really know and what's really in their hearts, and it involves them in the process of discovery, enabling them to remember and learn better.

Jesus set goals and objectives.

If people have no specific goals or outcomes, they will never know if they have succeeded. If people have no vision or mission, they are clueless and have no idea what their final destination is supposed to be. In contrast, when Jesus began His ministry in Nazareth, the first thing He did was announce His vision statement, which is found in the words of the prophet Isaiah (Isa. 61:1–2; Luke 4:18). Furthermore, Jesus operated with objectives and goals that enabled Him to fulfill His mission and vision with a daily understanding of what, when, and how to function (Luke 13:32).

Jesus invested time with those who bore fruit.

The Pareto Principle teaches us that 80 percent of the work done is accomplished by only 20 percent of the people in any given church or organization.[2] Jesus understood this principle long before Pareto. Jesus was wise and invested most of His time with disciples who bore much fruit instead of with the crowds. John 15:1–7 shows that Jesus expected His followers to bear much fruit if they abided in Him. He knew that He would get the most results by pouring into a few rather than focusing on the many. Although He ministered to the crowds, the Gospels clearly show that He invested most of His time with His twelve apostles and then the seventy disciples (Luke 9:1; 10:1).

Jesus confronted superficial religion.

Jesus did not like superficial religion and attacked religious leaders who misrepresented the heart of His Father (Matt. 23). He insisted that religious leaders allow God to first cleanse the inner man before focusing on outward rituals and religion (Matt. 23:26; Mark 7:15). Jesus also taught that religious tradition often nullifies the word of

God (Mark 7:13). Since He confronted superficial religion instead of placating it, He was able to raise up powerful men of God who demonstrated the truth with signs and wonders (Acts 3:6–7).

Jesus was able to tap into the fact that most people desire genuine faith and a true relationship with God and others. They are not interested in mere superficial rituals and religious performance. Even the young generation of today is sick and tired of phony performance based on institutional religion. They crave real, Christ-centered relationships and faith communities.

Jesus confronted political power.

When Jesus was with Pilate, He confessed that His primary purpose was to be recognized as the King (John 18:37). He was not afraid of offending those loyal to Caesar (which is the main reason He was crucified). He understood that the things that ruled external culture had to be shifted to another king and different gatekeepers if true systemic change was going to take place. Furthermore, He told Pilate that the power of His kingdom did not emanate from Rome but from His Father, God (v. 36). Jesus did not say that His kingdom is not *in* this world but that it was not *of* this world.

Even people in society today crave a faith that is relevant in the public square, something that is practical, not merely mystical. If we preach and demonstrate a faith in Christ that can positively influence the world around us, the next generation will come to our churches in droves.

Jesus was motivated by compassion.

Jesus did not heal merely to demonstrate His lordship but because He was moved by compassion (Mark 1:41). He was great in part because He had empathy and connected to the pain of those around Him (Heb. 4:15). Any leader without strong feelings of love for his people will not be motivated to serve and release them to greatness. People are not looking for just another church program. They are hungry for those who will pour into them and help them discover who they are and how they can fulfill their calling in life.

Jesus was willing to die for His purpose.

Life is not worth living if there is no transcendent purpose worth dying for. Jesus not only believed in His mission but was also willing to die on the cross in order to fulfill it (Heb. 12:2). Consequently He was able to instill and inspire such passion in His followers that most of the original twelve apostles died a martyr's death while preaching the gospel.[3] Truly the seed of the early church was the blood of the first- and second-century martyrs. Even today, two thousand years later, thousands of Christ followers continue to die for the cause of Christ, which is the main reason that Christianity became the largest and most formidable movement in the history of the world!

Releasing Greatness

There are some practical principles we can apply from the life of Christ in our quest to release greatness in others. In review of the Gospels we can say that without a doubt

Jesus' main focus in His earthly ministry was not preaching, teaching, healing, or ministering to the multitudes, but in pouring into His twelve men and making them His disciples.

In the New Testament the word *disciple* was used to describe Christ's followers much more than the word *Christian*. Jesus commands the church to make disciples, not just evangelize the lost (Matt. 28:19). Despite this lopsided focus, discipleship is not always the norm in the contemporary church. The following eleven indispensable principles are things I have learned as a pastor and disciple-maker for almost four decades.

Learn to be a spiritual parent.

In this day and age of broken families many new believers have no reference for submitting to authority, understanding a Father's love, keeping a covenant, and having a godly household. Since the church is a family of families and functions as the household of God, a primary function of a church in certain contexts should be to "re-parent" new believers, which is usually a very long process. Consequently in order to make disciples, we have to sometimes function as a spiritual parent more than merely a dispenser of biblical truth.

Don't focus on crowds, marketing, and budgets.

Many contemporary churches primarily focus on gathering crowds through marketing and providing a great Sunday experience. However, in order to make disciples, churches need to prioritize pouring into serious believers who are committed to the cause of Christ. The church will advance the kingdom through a holy minority, not through a compromised majority!

Be people oriented more than program based.

Discipleship cannot be done merely with an institutional program. It cannot take place only from the pulpit or with a weekly event. Not only did Paul the apostle preach the gospel; he also poured his life into the disciples. Disciples do life together, not just attend meetings and Bible studies together.

Consequently one of the most successful things I do to make disciples is have certain men travel with me when I minister so we can spend time hanging out and so they can observe how I interact and minister to those outside of our Sunday church context. I have found that spending quality time with a man for one week during a ministry trip is equal to six months of them going to weekly Bible studies; hence, it greatly accelerates their spiritual development.

Have a relational more than an institutional paradigm.

Along with the previous point, serious discipleship involves a very informal approach with those being mentored and does not merely rely upon formal church structures. Many pastors attempt to make disciples merely by sending potential leaders away to Bible school or by creating a Bible institute within their church. These methods may be good for giving people head knowledge but will not produce mature spiritual sons and daughters. Giving head knowledge without a personal connection affirms a worldly construct that can result in creating gifted leaders without godly character. Many of these models produce church splits because unproven leaders are installed who have no integrity.

Adopt the New Testament pattern for church life.

The New Testament pattern for church involves a lead pastor who is committed to one region until enough leaders are raised up to maintain the congregation. The assignment of the lead pastor is based upon the leading of the Lord and not politics and bureaucracy. The New Testament model for church also makes room for elders and deacons to be developed in addition to the lead pastor; hence, the lead pastor doesn't have to do all the work of the ministry. Furthermore, the New Testament also teaches that the body of Christ should be built up in love by that which every member supplies (Eph. 4:15–16) so that ministry is not relegated merely to professional clergy. All this makes room for discipleship because it leaves the door wide open for people to mature in Christ through serving God's household and beyond.

Espouse church life rather than a religious church culture.

Many church contexts are so religious that they don't engender genuine relationships necessary for discipling others. Religious cultures in congregations produce superficial relationships, church politics, and hypocrisy in the followers rather than true disciples. Since we cannot disconnect the relational dynamic from disciple making, a religious spirit is one surefire way to hinder a disciple-making culture in a congregation.

Focus on developing godly character more than promoting talented individuals.

Many churches are tempted to elevate carnal singers, musicians, and gifted preachers to fill a need in their congregation. However, in order to nurture mature disciples, the church needs to focus on developing Christlike character before a person is allowed to minister in public. When we allow spiritual babes to function in a leadership position, they can be tempted to be lifted up with pride and fall into a satanic snare (1 Tim. 3:5–7).

Develop leadership teams to anchor the lead pastor.

Many lead pastors focus on putting out fires, visiting the sick, and counseling the wounded as well as handling much of the management of the congregation. In addition to all this, they are expected to preach once or twice per week.

This leaves the pastor with no energy to pour into potential leaders and stymies the disciple-making process. Consequently the only way a church can regularly produce disciples is by the lead pastor focusing on building leadership teams who will bear the burden of the ministry with him so that they can focus on the ministry of the Word, disciple making, and prayer (Acts 6:2–4). Apart from having strong leadership teams around lead pastors, discipleship is almost impossible.

Adopt the father-son wineskin to counter the orphan spirit in the churches.

The Trinitarian model of Father, Son, and Spirit is the biblical model for oneness, unity, and households. In light of this, both the Old and New Testaments are models of a household of households under the leadership of the elders (or fathers). Hebrews 1:1 teaches that the prophets spoke in time past to the fathers, not the kings or priests, because the fathers had ultimate earthly authority. In the New Testament the qualification for elders (or spiritual leaders) was to be able to manage their own households well (1 Tim. 3:5), not to be great preachers. Why? Because the church is organically a household of households, or a family of families, just as the nation of Israel was in the Old Testament; hence, the church needs to adopt this father-son wineskin. The Holy Spirit functions maternally as the Comforter of the church. This is the only model the church can function in that has the power to break the orphan spirit over potential disciples who cannot function optimally until their generational curses of fatherlessness are broken (Mal. 4:6).

Practice consistent corporate prayer for spiritual vibrancy in the church.

Over the years, I have observed that the most significant disciples I developed had an intense hunger to seek God, not just say their prayers. Spirit-led prayer opens the individual up to the Spirit of God, who deposits into that person divine passion, power, and guidance. Since Jesus only ministered through the Holy Spirit (Acts 1:1–2), true disciples are those trained and endowed by the Spirit to minister. The best way to learn how to pray is by participating in powerful prayer meetings. Prayer is caught rather than taught. Acts 1 illustrates how the early church was birthed and empowered by an elongated time of seeking and waiting upon God. If the early church lived and breathed prayer to release kingdom purpose, how can today's church ever expect to produce culture-shifting disciples apart from fervent prayer? (See James 5:16–18.)

Build upon the local church paradigm rather than the parachurch paradigm for disciple making.

Finally, there are many well-meaning parachurch ministries who attempt to make disciples apart from the participation of the local church. They are strong regarding mission but weak regarding ecclesiology. They probably subconsciously reason, "Jesus made twelve disciples before there was a church, so we can do the same." However, even a cursory reading of the Gospels shows that the church was always the objective of Jesus' disciple-making plans. (See John 14–17 as an example.) As one who lived within the Trinitarian Father-Son wineskin, Jesus knew the only way to advance His kingdom was by producing a family of families that would eventuate in fulfilling the promise the Father made to Abraham—that in him all the families of the earth would be blessed (Gen. 12:1–3). Hence, the original cultural mandate would be fulfilled by empowering spiritual and biological families (Gen. 1:27–28). Of course this involves a lot more than just getting men together for a weekly Bible study. I have learned that unless a person's biologically family is connected to a spiritual family of families, its capacity to release God's purpose will be greatly limited.

Chapter 7

Walking in Your Assignment

*O*NE OF THE biggest fallacies in the church is that a believer can be anything he or she wants to be. Philippians 4:13, which says, "I can do all things through Christ who gives me strength" (BSB), is sometimes taken out of context to mean that a believer can decide to become or do whatever she desires. However, the passage is referring to Paul continuing with his ministry in spite of the financial challenges his ministry faced. If a believer can somehow be or do anything she wants, then Jesus would have ordained thousands of people as His apostles so more churches could be planted. But after spending all night in prayer, He chose only twelve to serve the kingdom as apostles. His choice of the twelve was not based on any biological or psychological traits, or because they were in proximity to Him. His choice was based on the calling of God and the gifts and abilities He saw in those twelve men. Hence, the Father had certain criteria that had to be met in order for His Son to ordain a person.

Although we don't know much about the background of some of the apostles, one thing they possibly all had in common was the fact that they were working in the marketplace. Some of them had their own fishing businesses—James, John, Andrew, and Peter (Matt. 4:18–22); one was a tax collector (Matt. 9:9); and another, Simon the Zealot, was involved in politics (Mark 3:18). Jesus didn't choose lazy people who were just sitting around doing nothing. He primarily chose men who were active in the business community, people who were at least busy using their gifts and abilities. Interestingly enough, there is no direct record of Him choosing a Levite, priest, or religious leader to be an apostle.

As a pastor I have learned that if you want to get something done, give it to the busiest people in the church! Because the needs of church and family are great, those who have a lot of free time are usually people who are lazy and shirk responsibility. So one of the most important things to think about when you are considering who you should attempt to mentor is whether that person is already faithful with the tasks in front of him or her. If a person cannot be faithful with the material things in this life, who is going to entrust to that person true riches? If a person cannot be faithful serving another person, who will entrust to him or her their own possessions to steward? (So said Jesus in Luke 16:10–12.)

Another of the greatest hindrances to people walking in the highest level of their potential is if they attempt to succeed in an area outside of their calling and giftings. God gave every person specific assignments in His kingdom based on their gifts and abilities. Therefore, if we walk outside of His assignment, we will not maximize our God-given potential. One of the saddest days in eternity will be when believers stand before the judgement seat of Christ and find out that they didn't do what God called them to do either because of fear of failure, unbelief, or laziness, or because they worked hard at succeeding in an area of work they were never called to (2 Cor. 5:10). Truly, productive, purposeful living doesn't come from mere activity or time management but from attention management related to our primary assignment in life.

In the past thirty years I have met numerous people who were deceived into thinking that they were called to sing (without any talent in that area) or were called to be pastors or ministers, although they had no grace or fruit to back up their claims. To reach our potential in life, we have to be honest with ourselves and not try to do something or be somebody that we are not called to do or be.

The great news is that God fearfully and wonderfully made each one of us (Ps. 139:13–14) and that there has never been and there will never be another you in all eternity! You (and every other person ever born) need to rest in the fact that you are more valuable than all the precious metals, stones, and jewels in the world because there is only one of you out of billions of people on the earth. Jesus said that our soul is worth more than the whole world. (See Mark 8:36.) I am not trying to be the next T. D. Jakes because I know that I can never be like T. D. in the same way that he can never be me. The more I accept who I am, the easier it will be for me to develop self-awareness, resulting in all my gifts and abilities being released on the earth.

Regarding our uniqueness, we have to remember that since God fashioned us while in our mothers' wombs, His work did not only begin in us post-conversion but started in us pre-birth, according to scriptures such as Psalm 139, Jeremiah 1:5, and Ephesians 1:4. The natural gifts, abilities, and personality, and the way we are wired emotionally, mentally, and physically, all have a part in determining our purpose in life. Thus, our natural abilities, person-alities, and gifts have to line up with our spiritual and motivational gifts in order to determine our purpose and unleash our potential.

As was already mentioned, if we feel God has called us to sing for Him, then we can correctly assume God will not only anoint us when we sing but grant us a special voice that is pleasing to the ear. If somebody feels God has called him to play for the NBA, to use it as a platform to preach the gospel, then said person better have the natural height, athleticism, and corresponding ability, as well as a track record in high school and college to fit the trajectory of a professional basketball player.

In other words, God is not stupid. If He appoints people to do something, He will not only anoint them but also equip them with both the spiritual and natural abilities necessary to perform the assignment. Consequently it is absolutely essential we have divine wisdom and an intuitive sense of how to prepare and place people properly for their calling if we are going to aid them in unleashing their potential. If we try to make everyone a preacher, or a singer, or in our own image, we will frustrate, discourage, and even destroy the faith of those we are setting up for failure.

Of course in the context of Luke 6:12-13 Jesus spent all night in prayer, which means we as mentees are responsible to hear from God regarding where we are to place those we are equipping. In the beginning stages every person should be involved in the ministry of helps—that is to say, to help in the material, menial things needed before the person is given anything of more importance. This is a great testing ground that enables mentors to test and develop those they are mentoring to see what kind of abilities, faithfulness, and attitude people have.

Even Jesus tested and trained His twelve apostles this way. For example, before He called them to function as apostles, they were operating as deacons, doing such things as helping sit people in groups of fifty and one hundred when Jesus was feeding the five thousand (Mark 6:33-44), buying Him food as He ministered to the spiritual needs of others (John 4), getting Him a donkey to ride upon (Luke 19:29-35), preparing the Upper Room for His last supper (Luke 22:8-13), and so on.

God–The Great Delegator

I heard it once said that the key to creating a movement is the distribution of labor. I believe that is true. The Bible speaks about the divine distribution of labor that has resulted in the largest, most powerful movement in the history of the world the past two millennia—Christianity. In both Corinthians and Romans we find some of what Scripture says about this divine distribution of labor.

The spiritual gifts (1 Cor. 12:4-6)

Paul the apostle teaches us in the first epistle to the Corinthians how there are a variety of gifts but the same Spirit, there are varieties of ministries but the same Lord, and there are varieties of manifestations or effects but the same God who works in all persons. So we see here that God takes varieties of gifts, ministries, and manifestations of the Spirit inside individual believers and distributes their labor in the church as He sees fit.

The spiritual manifestations (1 Cor. 12:7-10)

Paul also mentions nine different manifestations of the Spirit that operate in various individuals that God grants for the common good of all.

The nine gifts mentioned can be broken down into three categories:

1. The spoken gifts of tongues, interpretation of tongues, and prophecy

2. The revelatory gifts of the words of wisdom, knowledge, and discerning of spirits

3. The power gifts of healing, miracles, and faith

All these gifts are divine, momentary gifts that come upon a person and are not to be confused with residual abilities such as the wisdom a person has accumulated in life's experience or knowledge a person has acquired by reading books or the faith a person has developed by hearing and obeying the Word of God, as shown in 2 Thessalonians 1:3. The purpose of this chapter is not to explain each of these gifts and functions but to demonstrate how God places people in the church in a way that each individual member can have a part in showcasing a certain aspect of the working of God in the church and the world.

The ministry gifts in the church (1 Cor. 12:28)

Paul then mentioned (seemingly in hierarchical order) what order he places ministry gift leaders in the church, telling us that God has appointed in the church first apostles, second prophets, third teachers, then miracles, then gifts of healings, helps, and administrations. Hence, God is very practical, as He joins ministry gift teams together with those who have the ministry of helps and administration. Consequently it is not enough for a church to have anointed ministry leaders. It also has to have people operating in strong serving gifts and administration to harness the anointing to be an effective congregation.

Paul's teaching in this part of Corinthians is similar to another cluster of ministry gifts Jesus sent the church, as found in Paul's letter to the church in Ephesus. In his letter to the Ephesians, Paul says that God has also given the church some to be apostles, some to be prophets, some to be evangelists, and some to be pastors and teachers, to equip the saints for the work of the ministry for building up of the body of Christ (Eph. 4:11–12).

Hence, in this list apostles and prophets are also first and second, but instead of evangelist, teacher is listed third. Then, instead of using the word *evangelist*, healings and miracles are mentioned, which some say is another way of saying *evangelist* since the biblical evangelist (as seen in Philip's ministry to Samaria in Acts 8) is wrought with great signs and wonders and healings. Also, some have argued that in Ephesians the original Greek language shows pastor-teacher as one hyphenated function. Hence, all five are mentioned differently in both lists of ministry gifts (1 Cor. 12:28; Eph. 4:11).

Also notice that the purpose of these cluster gifts as found in Ephesians is not to do the work of the ministry but to help equip and place the saints for the work of the ministry (4:12), showing that the primary call of every so-called fivefold minister or every ministry gift is to be a mentor-equipper, not merely a preacher-minister.

Motivational gifts (Rom. 12:3-8)

Finally, Paul enumerates one more list worth noting if we are going to understand how to place people properly in the church. Paul starts off the way I started off this chapter, saying that we need not think more highly of ourselves than we ought to think, but with self-awareness and sobriety in order to understand the gifts God has given us according to our measure of faith.

Then Paul lists what many term "motivational gifts" to distinguish them from the gifts mentioned in his other epistles (1 Cor. 12; Eph. 4) since they seem to also be lumped together with things that are clearly motivational and residual (e.g., mercy and giving to others financially). These motivational gifts are to be distinguished from the manifestations of the Spirit mentioned in 1 Corinthians 12, such as the word of knowledge and wisdom. Note it does not say the encyclopedia or message of wisdom and knowledge. These manifestations of the Spirit are clearly meant to be fragmentary experiences of a divine bestowal of His grace for a specific time and task.

The motivational gifts mentioned show how God has hardwired individual believers in the church so that they are motivated to function in a certain way with a particular gift.

The gifts listed here are:

- Prophecy: Some have a prophetic motivation, not just a gift of prophecy, that comes upon them at times, as found in 1 Corinthians 12; 14.

- Service

- Teaching

- Exhortation

- Giving: Since all are commanded to give tithes and offerings, this is referring to a person highly motivated and assigned by God to create wealth for the kingdom to give to support the gospel.

- Leadership

- Mercy: Since all believers are called to have compassion for other people, this is obviously referring to a person who is motivated by a mercy gift, who will most likely have a strong compassionate outreach or ministry that aids other people continually as opposed to showing mercy once in a while as an opportunity arises.

In summary, according to Paul, we have various administrations and distributions of nine manifestations of the Spirit (1 Cor. 12), along with seven motivational gifts (Rom. 12) that come through the whole body of Christ under the leadership of the five cluster gifts (Eph. 4:11). We are called to recognize these gifts in people so they can equip them and properly place them (v. 12).

Finally, as we all do what God has called us to do, all will be edified, all will be blessed, and there will be a place for everyone in the church to minister, because it takes the whole body to function properly to release each individual part (1 Cor. 12:12–27).

Chapter 8

The Power of Failure

ONE OF THE great human freedoms is the freedom to fail and to get back up and try again! I have heard it said that before Abraham Lincoln became president of the United States, he went bankrupt and lost several local and national elections. To unleash potential, we must be willing to allow people to fail forward. Controlling others does not unleash their potential; trusting them to make mistakes and learn from those mistakes does.

Jesus was able to release potential better than anybody else, even though He had to work with people who were crude, unpolished, inexperienced leaders who often made mistakes. This was because Jesus allowed people to fail as part of their discipleship process. If Jesus were a micromanaging control freak who expected perfection from His followers, He would have failed in His mission of starting a global movement. We can see from reading the Gospels how all of His key people were entrusted with leadership even though they had a lot of rough edges and even failed when it came to some decision-making. For example, Jesus had to correct the apostles James and John for wanting to call fire down from heaven to destroy the city of Samaria because its inhabitants didn't want to receive Jesus (Luke 9:51–56).

The apostle Peter was initially so unpredictable that within a span of minutes he went from being the first person to receive the revelation from God the Father that Jesus was the promised Messiah to attempting to talk this Messiah out of fulfilling His main mission of dying on the cross for the sins of the world. Jesus actually addressed Peter as Satan because he was under the influence of the evil one (Matt. 16:13–23). In one episode Peter went from being influenced by God to a spokesperson for the devil!

Most of us probably would have given up on a person so unpredictable. But Jesus hung in there with Peter. After His ascension, Jesus used Peter as the spokesperson of His church even after Peter gave in to temptation and denied that he ever knew Jesus (Matt. 26:69–75). Consequently Jesus restored Peter back to ministry after He rose from the dead (John 21:15–17) and was proved correct, because in just a few short weeks Peter became the leader of the newly formed church and preached that great message on the day of Pentecost that led to three thousand people committing themselves to following Christ!

I remember when I first started our ministry in 1980. We had a young man fresh out of Bible school who had an incredible heart for God and felt a call to preach the gospel. He had a lack of confidence, which manifested through excessive stuttering. Even though he could hardly get a sentence out of his mouth without stuttering, I allowed him to preach on occasion and kept encouraging him despite his obvious limitations. I never told him that he stuttered, and despite how painful it was in those beginning days to hear him preach, the Lord kept showing me to have him preach. He began to transform right before my eyes and within a few years rarely stuttered. He eventually moved to another country with his family and did such powerful missionary work that a whole nation was greatly impacted by his ministry to the leaders of the church in that island nation!

To this day he has a strong and viable ministry that would have been in jeopardy if I would have corrected him for his excessive stuttering and told him that he couldn't preach unless he overcame his speech impediment. Most people forget that Michael Jordan, arguably the greatest basketball player of all time, was cut from his high school team and didn't win his first (of six) championships with the Chicago Bulls until he was twenty-eight years old and in the league for about seven years! The Bulls became so dominant that most people thought that winning a championship was automatic for them, but they had to suffer many years of failure in the playoffs before they reached their potential.

Failure can actually lead to success and to the release of our potential when we can learn from our past and become wiser for the future. When we learn from our experiences, those experiences become a tool for us to grow. If we refuse to honestly assess our life and learn from our failures, we are doomed to keep repeating the same mistakes over and over and will waste years of our lives. We need to view failure in the same way that scientists view it. While our American culture glorifies success and loves its winners, as illustrated in how we worship our sports heroes, the greatest advances in science and technology came about in Western history because scientists viewed failure in an experiment as just another process in their journey of proving their hypothesis. Thus, every failure was a continuum to build upon because it narrowed down the possibilities and got closer to finding the true hypothesis. If we would only view failure as scientists do instead of how it's viewed in sports (with a winner-take-all approach), then we would continually advance in our quest toward releasing our potential in life.

Another way of viewing failure in a positive light is by realizing that sometimes we fail because we are taking on new and greater responsibilities that challenge our mental, spiritual, and physical abilities. For example, powerlifters will attempt to lift a weight they have never successfully lifted before in order to increase their capacity for muscle strength and resistance. In doing this, they will often fail to lift it by themselves, but they will have a person spotting them who will aid them by placing a finger on the weight to help them complete a full repetition. If they only lifted weights they were comfortable with and didn't push their muscles to failure, they would never go to the next level. When I first learned how to ride a bike, I continually fell for three days before I was able to successfully keep my balance and ride. A baby has to fall numerous times before he or she learns to walk and has to master walking before he or she can ever begin to run.

I was encouraging a man who was discouraged because he thought he was losing ground in his faith and back-sliding because he was failing in some of the tests and temptations that were coming his way. I told him that he wasn't losing ground spiritually because now he had more responsibility than ever before and was failing merely because the tests were getting harder and harder and revealing weaknesses in his character that he had to overcome by continuing to mature. We have to remember that when we come to a new level, there will be a new and greater devil to meet us and test us!

Amazingly enough, as I finished writing this chapter, I came across an interview with Nick Foles, the quarterback of the Philadelphia Eagles. He said things in the article that line up with the principles in this chapter. I want to quote some excerpts of his interview:

> "I think the big thing is don't be afraid to fail," Foles said. "I think in our society today, Instagram, Twitter, it's a highlight reel. It's all the good things. And then when you look at it, when you think like, wow, when you have a rough day, 'My life's not as good as that,' (you think) you're failing.
>
> "Failure is a part of life. It's a part of building character and growing. Without failure, who would

you be? I wouldn't be up here if I hadn't fallen thousands of times. Made mistakes.

"We all are human, we all have weaknesses, and I think throughout this, (it's been important) to be able to share that and be transparent. I know when I listen to people speak and they share their weaknesses, I'm listening. Because (it) resonates.

"So I'm not perfect. I'm not Superman. I might be in the NFL, I might have just won a Super Bowl, but, hey, we still have daily struggles, I still have daily struggles. And that's where my faith comes in, that's where my family comes in.

"I think when you look at a struggle in your life, just know that's just an opportunity for your character to grow. And that's just been the message. Simple. If something's going on in your life and you're struggling? Embrace it. Because you're growing."[1]

To summarize what I have learned about failure in life, the following are twelve principles I want to leave with you as I end this chapter. These principles are essential if we are going to have the attitude necessary to both teach and release people to unleash their potential and walk in their divine destiny. Why? Because everybody will be tested by failure—some more than others. How people react and respond to personal failure will determine whether they will be ordinary or extraordinary in life.

Fail Forward

I heard it said once that "failure is the parent of innovation." This is a very true statement because before every successful career or endeavor there are usually a multitude of failures.

We all have to learn to fail forward. Anytime we enter a new year, we should reflect on the successes and failures of the past year, using both as a trajectory toward a more productive experience for the future. By success I am referring to living a life that bears fruit to the glory of God. By failure I mean anything we initiated or participated in that did not bring glory to the name of Jesus or bear any immediate, noticeable fruit. Failure can also be defined as when a paradigm, strategy of life, or ministry is no longer producing the results we set out to obtain.

On January 10, 2019, I celebrated my anniversary as a believer and follower of Jesus Christ. I have served in official full-time church ministry since November 1980; hence I have had to deal consistently with numerous people with a plethora of challenges in the context of a complex metropolis like New York City. During these years, I have been through many stages and cycles of life and have experienced both success and failure. I have learned the hard way to embrace failure as part of the normal process of learning. The older I get, the more experience I have, and hopefully the less intense lessons of failure I need to experience in my life journey.

Since Christ is the redeemer of all failure and sin, the

Bible is replete with success stories and has a narrative that involves utilizing failure and evil for good. For example, after the patriarch Joseph was sold as a slave by his biological brothers, many years later he was providentially promoted to second in command in Egypt. After encountering Joseph as their political leader, his siblings feared his retribution. Yet Joseph told them that what they meant for evil God meant for good (Gen. 50:20). The apostle James wrote that we should count it pure joy when we fall into diverse trials because the outworking of these tests develops our character (Jas. 1:2–4). Furthermore, Jesus' suffering resulted in His glorious resurrection (Phil. 2:5–11). No matter what the devil tries to do, God outdoes him and turns the tables on him!

Thus, the Bible has a theology of success that can come out of any failure we experience, if we respond to God in faith and humility. Furthermore, Romans 8:28 teaches us that all things work together for good for those who love God. One of the greatest discoveries I have made is that I can't lose as a Christ follower. Even when I fail, I can seize failure as an opportunity for further growth so I can go to another level of success!

Every situation and circumstance, no matter how difficult, can be redeemed for good! We have to realize that since all of us are sinners who fall short of the glory of God, failure of some sort is inevitable for every one of us. This does not mean that we stop trying to succeed or have a defeatist mentality; it merely means we have to have the right perspective if we are going to break through to success.

As a case in point, Abraham Lincoln—arguably the greatest president—had a long list of failures on his resume before he actually made it to the top. The following was his path to the presidency:

- He failed in business at age 21.

- He was defeated in a legislative race at age 22.

- He failed again in business at age 24.

- He overcame the death of his sweetheart at age 26.

- He had a nervous breakdown at age 27.

- He lost a congressional race at age 34, he lost another congressional race at age 36, and he lost a senatorial race at age 45.

- He did not become vice president at age 47, and he lost a senatorial race at age 47.

- To the shock and surprise of many, he was elected president of the United States at age 52.[2]

Psalm 37:23–24 says, "The steps of a man are established by the LORD, when he delights in his way; though he fall, he shall not be cast headlong, for the LORD upholds his hand." Proverbs 24:16 says, "A just man falls seven times and rises up again" (MEV).

Anybody who thinks he will be exempt from severe tests and failure just because he serves God is mistaken. All you have to do is read the Book of Psalms, which is replete with the stories of people who have experienced both failure and success, along with emotional depression and exultant joy. In light of this it is extremely important for every person to understand how to turn every failure into (eventual) success.

Twelve Ways to Turn Failure Into Success

1. Change what you say to yourself.

The first and foremost thing we must do after failure is pick ourselves back up. The way to do this is to shut out every negative voice inside our heads. Entertaining negative thoughts will result in hopelessness, discouragement, and even depression. The importance of this cannot be overstated. Proverbs 23:7 says, "As he thinks in his heart, so he is" (MEV). We become the accumulation of our thoughts since thoughts lead to actions and actions lead to habit patterns, which then determine our destiny. The longer we wallow in this kind of "stinking thinking," the harder it will be to climb out of our emotional pit. Since we speak to ourselves more than we speak to anybody else, it is vitally important that we control what we think.

In Numbers 13:33 we see that the children of Israel thought that they were like grasshoppers compared with the giants in the Promised Land. This filled them with unbelief and caused a whole generation to miss the purpose of God! We need to change our internal conversations and tell ourselves that "we are more than conquerors through him who loved us" (Rom. 8:37) and that we can do all things through Christ who strengthens us (Phil. 4:13). We also need to make a commitment to only speak and think words that release faith, truth, and purpose. Philippians 4:8 tells us, "Whatever is true, whatever is honorable, whatever is just, whatever is pure, whatever is lovely, whatever is commendable, if there is any excellence, if there is anything worthy of praise, think about these things." We could all do well and recover from any failure if we would only obey this passage.

2. Learn from your past mistakes.

If scientists and innovators in technology treated failure the way most people do, then scientific and technological progress would be stifled! Those in fields of research understand that for every failed experiment, they are closer to proving or disproving their hypotheses. Failure should always serve as a catalyst to get us to recalibrate how we operate and make us more efficient. Even the corrections in the market economy during the past several years are part of a normal cycle of allowing what really works to come to the fore and correct some of the systemic ills regarding our cultural business habits. What does this all mean? Failure is the natural process of learning to be successful—only if we reflect and learn from the mistakes that lead to failure.

3. Examine your priorities.

One of the greatest lessons I have learned in life is the realization that knowing what *not* to do is just as important as knowing what to do. Many gifted people I know never accomplish anything of substance because they are scattered and not focused. Their schedules are always filled with numerous activities from morning till evening. For example, I receive numerous opportunities and invitations to minister locally, nationally, and internationally. If I took every good opportunity that came my way, even those that seem to fit my mission and purpose in life, I would lose my center of gravity and become less effective in my key relationships in family and ministry.

I have learned that it is a mistake to equate mere activity with significance. Failure has helped shape my core priorities in life that are centered in seeking God, personal study, family relationships, and mentoring key and emerging leaders. Everything else has to take a back seat. Be true to your core values and prioritize everything in your life around them. Do not allow yourself to participate in things that are not Spirit-led and are contrary to the most important things in your life. Of course this does not mean that we only do things we like; that would be narcissistic and self-serving.

We all have unexpected things that invade our lives and interfere with our normal schedules. When unexpected things happen, just be faithful, fulfill your responsibilities, and get back on track as soon as possible. Don't let emergencies get you out of your divine rhythm and into bad habit patterns. The apostle Paul said it best: "Look carefully then how you walk, not as unwise but as wise, making the best use of the time, because the days are evil; Therefore do not be foolish, but understand what the will of the Lord is" (Eph. 5:15–17).

4. Surround yourself with spiritually mature people.

As a young leader, I hoped God was going to use me to bring great revival to New York City. But several years into our young ministry I went to hell and back (figuratively) and experienced much suffering due to failures in my own key relationships and ministry. After several years of intense trauma I came out of these trials with an understanding of how much I needed to relate to my peers in ministry. This resulted in an intense desire to network key leaders and churches from around the city, which gave birth to All City Prayer initiatives, starting in 1991, in which more than a thousand people and more than fifty churches and leaders would come together for a day of fasting and prayer for our city. That was followed by many other city-wide initiatives too numerous to mention. (Read my book *Kingdom Awakening* for more on these initiatives.) All of this was precipitated by my experiencing failure in multiple areas.

The greatest lesson I learned during that time (besides the faithfulness of God) is to surround myself with godly friends and mature believers with a passion for God who can lift me up when I am down and vice versa. Truly God said it is not good for a man to be alone (Gen. 2:18).

Scripture also says, "Two are better than one, because they have a good reward for their toil. For if they fall, one will lift up his fellow. But woe to him who is alone when he falls and has not another to lift him up. Again, if two lie together, they keep warm, but how can one keep warm alone? And though a man might prevail against one who is alone, two will withstand him—a threefold cord is not quickly broken" (Eccles. 4:9–12).

Many believers make the mistake of hanging out with people just because they attend the same church, but Paul, writing to Timothy in the context of the local church, told him to "pursue righteousness, faith, love, and peace, along with those *who call on the Lord from a pure heart*" (2 Tim. 2:22, emphasis added). Not every person in the church is good for you to hang out with when you are struggling with failure. Some will actually encourage your failure because it makes them feel good about their own shortcomings. Be careful, be selective, but pursue mature believers with a good track record who have proved themselves to be faithful and successful through the tough challenges in life. They are the only ones who can help lift you up to where you belong. I can always tell how successful people will be in the future by the kind of people they hang out with and include in their inner circle.

5. Get mentors who will help you get to the next level.

Ask God to provide you with a mentor who has already been where you desire to go, has weathered the storms of life, and has a proven track record. Every person needs a mentor, a person who will advise and keep him or her accountable in a specific area of life. Listening to the advice of a good mentor can save you years of learning and spare you from wasting precious time. Why reinvent the wheel? Remember, without Moses we would never have had a Joshua; without Elijah we would not have had Elisha; without the apostle Barnabas we may have never had an apostle Paul; without the apostle Paul we would never have had an apostle Timothy. (See Numbers 27:18–23; 1 Kings 19:19–21; Acts 9:26–27; and Acts 16:1–3.) Everybody needs somebody else to take him or her to where he or she needs to go.

6. Let your failures work godly character in you.

God has used failure to bring me closer to Him and help me rely upon Him more for my well-being, identity, and success. As a younger person I could only reach a certain point of humility on my own based on Bible reading and private devotion. God had to use the fiery trials of life experience that come through time to work a deeper level of humility in my soul. The worse thing we can do when we experience failure is blame other people for what happened. Doing this will stop the process of internal growth. The only people who grow and come out better on the other side of failure are those who have humbled themselves and taken responsibility for their part in failure. In hard times we can either get bitter or better, run from God or run to God. Remember, what happens *to* you is never as important as what happens *inside* you! Circumstances will never destroy you. It's how you respond to them that determines your destination in life.

Struggles with my own children and family have given me more compassion with Christian parents and spouses who have their own family challenges. If I did not have these challenges myself, it is highly likely I would have been judgmental toward those who have experienced family failure. Hence, my own struggles have produced in me the compassion necessary to empathize with others. Furthermore, I have found that I have far more authority to speak and minister to people in the areas where I have experienced the most challenges. My heart and emotions can now resonate with people who are going through the same battles I have experienced. Related to this, I have learned that the greatest point of demonic attack against me cues me to my greatest calling in life. Our greatest calling is always hidden beneath our greatest point of resistance and challenges. I have found that my mess can work compassion in me and become my message that can be a great benefit for others with the same struggles (2 Cor. 1:3–7). There is always a purpose for everything. Every failure can be a schoolmaster who prepares us to go to the next level of success and influence.

7. Become more self-aware and less defensive.

One of the benefits of failure is that it made me more aware of who I am and what really motivates me. I started to discover more acutely when I am being driven by fleshly, personal ambition and when the Lord is leading me. It is very important after or during a failure that we take the time to reflect and allow the Lord to reveal to us the things we did to contribute to the mess we are in. We need to realize when we are operating in presumption and running ahead of the Lord. Every time we experience failure, we should use it as an opportunity to self-reflect and learn how and why we did what we did so we do not repeat the same mistakes. Also, part of the process of becoming self-aware is to listen to the rebuke and correction of others God sends into our lives. The worst thing we can do after failure is isolate ourselves from others or become defensive when a person attempts to speak into our life. "A wise man will hear and increase learning" (Prov. 1:5) and "the wise in heart will receive commands" (Prov. 10:8).

8. Let your spirituality be grounded in reality.

Sometimes success can lead to failure. I have found that more people have fallen because of success than failure. This is because often when we go from one successful endeavor to another, we lose our sense of reality and begin to take things for granted (such as doing due diligence before making important decisions and making commitments to others). Failure shakes us up and brings us more to the ground level of how the world really operates. It can also be the impetus for acquiring more discernment for future decisions.

Also, some folks are so mystical in their approach to Christianity that they never take into consideration the realities, challenges, and complexities of their environment.

Not only are we called to pray; we are also called to think and act. We are called to have powerful encounters with God so we can successfully engage the earth in His power and might. Jesus did not stay on top of the Mount of Transfiguration. He came down to the valley to encounter the evil spirits that were afflicting humankind (Matt. 17:1–18). He was empowered and strengthened so He could successfully deal with the betrayal of His disciples, His agony in the Garden of Gethsemane, and endure the excruciating pain of the crucifixion.

He did not attempt to use prayer and spirituality to escape the realities of the earth. Instead, He depended upon His power encounters with the Father to obtain the wisdom and strength necessary to complete His purpose on the earth.

9. Share the lessons you learn through failure.

I spend a lot of time mentoring young people. Some of the most fruitful times I have in those sessions occur when I share my past failures and the reasons that led to them. Without these compelling stories I would not be equipped with the wisdom I need to encourage and exhort these younger, less experienced people. Don't waste your failure merely on yourself. Use these experiences to train the next generation and bless others with the lessons you have learned. Truly I have found that the teacher always learns more than the student. When we share our life lessons with others, it helps us gain more insight as well.

10. Learn to construct a better model for others to follow.

Ultimately our lives are our legacy. Consequently every failure should become a building block for us to construct a better model of how we live. Failure can force us to pause in this hectic world and grapple for balance and proper rhythm. It can enable us to see what really works as opposed to what is an unworkable concept.

When people with little experience have immediate success, it pains me to see them become mentors or coaches before they know if their model is sustainable over the long haul. For example, there are some pastors who have enormous church growth and are writing books and giving advice to a new generation of leaders, yet they lead local churches that are less than ten years old. This is too early to tell if their model can withstand the test of time regarding ministry burnout, leadership turnover, and multigenerational success in developing healthy families that will keep their children and perpetuate the faith. I don't believe we can trust models and philosophies of life or ministry until they have experienced the fiery trials of life and come out successfully on the other side.

11. Be motivated to grow in faith.

The Bible passage in Zechariah 4:6 is more real to me today than ever before. Truly I have found that when all is said and done, it is not by my power or might. It takes God's Spirit to accomplish His will and purpose in the earth. Failure has taught me the vast limitations of depending upon my natural gifts and abilities to fulfill my kingdom purpose. When I hit a wall and have no solutions, God reminds me that it is going to take faith in His ability to intervene and perform a miracle to accomplish His will!

12. Give God opportunity every day to instruct you.

The longer I live, the more I realize that I will never get the results I want in life without seeking God earnestly. We need to give God space to mold us and speak to us. I have found that when I initiate anything significant based solely on my own planning, natural gifts, and abilities, then it is up to me to keep it going on my own strength. God is not obligated to empower that which He never willed to exist! One of the greatest keys to Jesus' success was the fact that He only did what He saw His father doing (John 5:19).

The older I get, the more I try never to get involved in anything unless it fits my purpose and mission and is accompanied by a strong witness in my spirit of God's leading. Of course I have come to this conclusion after going through the school of hard knocks and almost suffering burnout on several occasions!

In conclusion, it is my objective to encourage you not to quit and to help you understand that failure is one of the key stepping-stones to success. I pray you will reflect on each of the twelve points presented here so you can apply these timeless truths to your life. If you do, I trust you will have a far greater chance of turning your failures into successes. The twelve points are essential guides to both mentor and mentee, to teacher and student, regarding the proper attitude to have when we experience failure. Failure is not the end of the world but may actually become the beginning of something great! I have found that every crisis is really a hidden opportunity for God to change our paradigms and give us solutions to challenges that we would have never received had everything been going great. Crisis that arises out of failure is also often the impetus for seeking God so that He can initiate changes in strategies, methods, and even our vocational plans.

As mature mentors devoted to releasing other people to their calling, we need to pour these principles into those who look to us so that they don't quit when the going gets tough and they experience failure. Teach them that failure may actually be the very thing that teaches the life lessons they need for long-term success.

Chapter 9

The Power of Delegation

NOT LONG AFTER Jesus chose twelve apostles out of His larger group of disciples (Luke 6:12–13), He gave them power and authority over all demons, and power to heal diseases. Then He sent them out to proclaim the kingdom of God and to heal (Luke 9:1–2). Clearly, Jesus understood what it meant to delegate responsibility (Luke 9:1–2; 10:1). In fact His goal was to work Himself out of a job!

In Luke 9:2 the phrase *sent out* is Greek *apostelló*, which means "send away or send out."[1] It is a compound word: *apo*, "from, away from,"[2] and *stéllō*, "make ready...dispatch...send."[3] This same word also occurs when Jesus sends out the seventy (Luke 10:1). Therefore, this means the word *sent* is not limited to the original twelve apostles but can be used regarding sending others. We see it used in other places in the New Testament (Acts 13:2). Hence, Jesus was taking the movement to another level instead of allowing it to be solely dependent upon Him. He delegated power and authority to others so that the movement could multiply.

Scripture shows the apostles receiving both power (Greek *dunamis*) and authority (Greek *exousia*). These are similar but different concepts:

- Power: *dunamis* means "power, might, strength...force...ability."[4] It refers to the raw power needed to accomplish a task.

- Authority: *exousia* refers to "authority, absolute power, warrant,"[5] "the power exercised by rulers or others in a high position by virtue of their office."[6]

For example, a police officer has the legal authority to stop a car but not the power to stop a car. A man with a gun may have the power to kill someone but not the legal authority to kill someone. Hence, *dunamis* is the raw power; *exousia* is the authority to use that power.

So we see the amazing truth that Jesus gave His apostles both the raw power and the legal authority to preach, heal, and cast out demons. Jesus has bestowed similar power and authority upon all believers, as we see in other passages, such as Mark 16:15–18 and James 5:14–15. We also see how, after they returned, they gave an account of everything they did to Jesus as a way to debrief, compare notes, and be corrected and encouraged, if need be. (See Luke 9:10.)

As the last Adam (1 Cor. 15:45), Jesus was now multiplying Himself even as the first Adam was commanded to do (Gen. 1:28). Of course the first Adam was only able to multiply himself biologically. Jesus, on the other hand, was multiplying Himself in spirit and truth. Given the fact that Jesus did not have that much time left on the earth, He was totally focused on increasing His ability to proliferate the teaching and the movement before He ascended into heaven. Consequently, after empowering only twelve of the disciples, we find that He appointed another seventy disciples to proclaim the kingdom and heal the sick (Luke 10:1–16).

These disciples also came back to give a report to Jesus, and we find them excited because even demons submitted to them in the name of Jesus (vv. 17–19). His response was to instruct them not to be excited about casting out demons but to be excited because their names were written in heaven (v. 20). As a master releaser of potential and a master at turning ordinary men into extraordinary leaders, Jesus understood that mere teaching was not enough to develop the potential in others. He knew that unless He gave them work to do, they would not continue to grow. Thus, His formula was something like this:

- Jesus would choose somebody to be with Him, to do life with Him, not just hear Him preach at religious gatherings.

- Jesus would give them time to bond with Him and with others on the team.

- Jesus would model leadership and ministry
  to them.

- Jesus would then send them out to do what
  He did once He felt they had enough training.

- Jesus would then call them aside to debrief,
  compare notes, and correct them as needed.

Once the initial team was established, Jesus expanded the group and repeated the same process so that the movement would have a larger base of leaders to perpetuate the kingdom of God. Jesus understood and demonstrated three important principles. One, the movement should never depend upon the leadership and abilities of one person. Two, those He was discipling would never grow with mere teachings and meetings. They had to be given responsibility to put the teachings into practice. Three, the movement could only grow and be sustained based on how large the leadership base underpinning it was.

In the same way, Jesus developed people and unleashed their potential through the principle of delegation and stewardship. We must do the same if we are going to have the same results. I have found that people can only grow through teaching in the initial six months to a year after they come to Christ. After that, unless they volunteer or serve in the church, they will not continue to grow. Jesus told His disciples that His food was to do the will of Him who sent Him (John 4:32–34). In other words, we are fed by "doing" the Word of God, not just by hearing the Word of God.

Therefore, it is essential that we who want to mature others in Christ learn to delegate responsibility to those we are mentoring. This engenders trust, gives an opportunity to see the strengths and weaknesses of the person you are mentoring, and gives you the ability to critique and hone the skills of your mentee.

This is the same method I followed with Kristian. After he was a believer for about a year, I started entrusting him with certain responsibilities in the church, which led to him becoming the youth leader about five years later. This gave me ample opportunity to speak into him, as well as develop his gifts and abilities as a biblical communicator and emerging leader. Taken together, all these things eventually led to Kristian becoming the lead pastor of his own congregation.

Three Stages of Mentoring Others

I have found that one of the most important things about delegation is to walk through three stages with those I am mentoring, to allow both for the growth of the individual and proper accountability in the process. Stage one involves giving the person you are mentoring some responsibility as part of his or her assignment. You give guidelines including goals, timelines, and objectives so that the person knows the overall mission of the task and the outcomes you are looking for. Stage two comes once the task is completed. It is then you have a time of meeting with your mentee to assess what was done, how it was done, and if the goals, objectives, and timelines were met. Stage three is the time for encouragement, correction, and fine-tuning before the person is ready for the next assignment, unless he or she failed to accomplish the task properly, in which case the person should be given another opportunity to attempt another assignment.

If any of these three stages is neglected, then you are not properly discipling new people, which in turn robs them of the opportunity to truly grow and release their potential. Consequently delegation does not mean merely giving out tasks without any follow-up or accountability, especially in a case when someone is given a new or unfamiliar task. Someone has to oversee the mentee closely in the initial stages and then debrief that person once the task is completed. The more familiar and experienced the person becomes with the assignment, the less oversight he or she will need and the more freedom that person should be given. Eventually we should get to a place where we just give guidelines to the person, along with timelines and goals, and then leave the person alone! While the overall mission remains the same, the ways in which the person accomplishes the mission and the methods he or she uses might be different from the teacher depending upon gifts, abilities, and personality.

Enabling people to have freedom within the guidelines is perhaps the greatest way to develop their skills and release them to being extraordinary people. Micromanaging, telling someone how to do things, and breathing over their shoulder after they have already been trained and proven, will only frustrate them and cause them to quit. Leaders who do not know how to train, delegate, and release others will cap the growth of their organization as well as the growth capacity of individuals they are attempting to mature as Christ followers.

I thank God my original pastor, Ben Crandell, was not afraid to allow me to grow into ministry as a young man. I had been a believer for only six months when I organized my first big evangelistic event in a New York City public park. Eventually I was put in charge of busing many people to our church as well as being the section leader of about twelve cell group leaders who met with me once per month for prayer and instruction. At this point I had been a believer for only about three years!

My pastor was not afraid to take chances with me even though I was only twenty-two years old when he first started giving me a lot of responsibility. However, it was through those formative years of organizing meetings, bus routes, and helping cell group leaders that I was able to hone my skills as an organizer, leader, and teacher, which enabled me to become a lead pastor by the time I was twenty-five years old. If my pastor had been insecure and unable to delegate responsibility to an unproven young emerging leader like me, I would have never grown as a leader and become equipped for what I am presently doing today. My personal experience illustrates the importance of delegation as part of the equipping process of unleashing potential in others. Without the process of delegation being incorporated into our discipleship processes, there is no practical matrix to demonstrate a person's growth and capacity. By growth I am referring not only to skill but also to character that will be tested in the midst of the assigned tasks.

To use an everyday example to further illustrate the three stages necessary for development, can you imagine the foolishness of giving a person a license to practice medicine or perform surgery just because the person received high academic grades in school? Imagine if a person could become a surgeon without first serving under another doctor as an intern? What if we gave people a license to drive a car just because they were able to pass the written permit test? Unfortunately the church has a history of ordaining people into full-time church ministry or even as lead pastors merely because they went away to a seminary and received a master of divinity. How foolish and unbiblical this is.

As we conclude this chapter, I truly believe that all our training and work here on the earth is ultimately preparing us for the day in which we will disciple whole nations as Jesus commanded in Matthew 28:19. The word *nations* here has to do with people groups, not merely an individual ethnic person. Paul alludes to this in his letter to the Corinthians when he chides the church by saying that one day the saints will judge angels (1 Cor. 6:3), so how much more should we be able to steward the matters belonging to this life? Thus, not only individual believers but whole churches are being prepared by God to steward the things of this world so that one day we will be entrusted with community building and shepherding nations! After all, we are joint heirs with Christ (Rom. 8:17), who has been commissioned by the Father to inherit the nations and the ends of the earth as His possession (Ps. 2). Consequently everything we delegate to another person and everything the Lord delegates to us is training ground for more responsibility that eventually will prepare us to rule and reign with the Lord Jesus (Rev. 2:26–27).

Chapter 10

The Power of Prioritizing

EVEN A CURSORY examination of the Gospels shows that Jesus favored certain individuals over others. That is to say, He intentionally invested more of His time with certain people. Even though He ministered to the crowds, out of them He had disciples—those who made a commitment to follow Him (Luke 14:25–26). Out of those disciples Jesus chose twelve (Luke 6:13), whose primary task was to spend time with Him (Mark 3:14) before they were sent out to preach and heal the sick. Hence, Jesus' main agenda on the earth was not ministering to the crowds but investing His time training the twelve. We also see by examining the Gospel narratives that out of the twelve Jesus had an inner circle of three: James, John, and Peter, who spent the most time with Him (Matt. 26:36–38). Out of those three it seemed as though John the son of Zebedee was the most intimate with Jesus (John 21:20).

Jesus followed what became famous in business-management philosophy and is known as the Pareto Principle:

> The Pareto principle (also known as the 80/20 rule, the law of the vital few, or the principle of factor sparsity) states that, for many events, roughly 80% of the effects come from 20% of the causes. Management consultant Joseph M. Juran suggested the principle and named it after Italian economist Vilfredo Pareto, who noted the 80/20 connection while at the University of Lausanne in 1896, as published in his first paper, *Cours d'économie politique*. Essentially, Pareto showed that approximately 80% of the land in Italy was owned by 20% of the population.
>
> It is an axiom of business management that "80% of sales come from 20% of clients." Richard Koch authored the book, *The 80/20 Principle*, which illustrated a number of practical applications of the Pareto principle in business management and life. Following Koch's seminal work, many business executives have cited the 80/20 rule as a tool to maximize business efficiency.[1]

In the vernacular this means that about 80 percent of the output of any organization is going to come from only about 20 percent of the people. I have found this to be true not only in business but in the church world. As a pastor,

I have observed that only about 20 percent of the people in the congregation give the bulk of the tithes and offerings and do the most volunteering in the church. This is just human nature; 80 percent of the people are just here for the ride, and only a remnant of about 20 percent truly believe the message of the gospel and put it into practice with all of their heart.

The apostle Paul also showed that he followed this principle when he instructed his protégé, Timothy, to pick out of the crowds faithful men who had the ability to teach and entrust the Word unto them (2 Tim. 2:2). When pastors or businesses merely focus on the crowds instead of targeting their attention on those most likely to bring back the biggest return on their investment of time, they are being unwise stewards and do not understand how to prioritize the way Jesus and Paul did.

As was already mentioned in a previous chapter, Jesus chose people with potential (all had their own businesses or were already busy in leadership) and did not waste His time with people who were lazy or who wanted to argue with Him. He did not spend most of His time with the religious leaders who opposed Him but with those who were hungry and thirsty for Him and who also had the most leadership potential.

Consequently this may come as a shock for those in the body of Christ who view the Bible with a democratic lens instead of theocratic lens, but God is not into egalitarianism! God does not treat every person equally. Some have a greater call than others, and some will have more divine encounters with God than other people. Also, not every person is called to be a fivefold minister (Eph. 4:11). Only some are called to function as fivefold ministry leaders in the church. Also, not every fivefold minister has the same measure of this gift of Christ. (See Ephesians 4:7, 11.)

The context of 2 Timothy 2:2 is that Paul, as an extra local leader—an apostolic leader—was pouring His time into Timothy as another extra local (apostolic) leader who in turn was encouraged by Paul to identify and invest his time with other potential extra local (apostolic) leaders who could in turn help lead other burgeoning congregations and plant new ones. Notice that in this passage Paul told Timothy to differentiate between those who heard the message in the midst of many witnesses and those who were faithful and able to teach others. Hence, he told Timothy to collapse the crowd into smaller segments of individual believers who had high-capacity potential so that Timothy could endeavor to invest in those high-capacity individuals and then release them into ministry. By focusing on the few instead of the crowd, Timothy was not being cruel but wise, because, as already mentioned, only about 20 percent of the people will do about 80 percent of the ministry. That is to say, by focusing on the faithful, able few rather than the many, there would be a greater chance for the movement to have a sustainable future because there would be more capable people able to minister and perpetuate the gospel message.

When I first started Resurrection Church in 1984, my motto and key method for building the church was based on the Paul-Timothy model of 2 Timothy 2:2. I started off selecting about eight men whom I met with once per week for a few hours. I called them my "Timothy group." Afterward, as the church grew, I met with about thirty men for three hours weekly and called it Men in Training (MIT). Eventually, about a year later, I met with them every other week and started another group of thirty men called the Junior MIT. For many years I met with these men. We went through books together, prayed together, and strategized together. They became my greatest leaders! Many of them (such as Kristian) became my elders, leaders, and pastors, and we sent out many of them to start churches or their own evangelistic mission. Truly the MIT became the cornerstone of Resurrection Church and the primary reason that since 1984 the church is still growing, expanding into other campuses, and nurturing and sending out high-end leaders to advance the kingdom of God!

Before we close out this chapter, I want us to examine more closely how Jesus chose His friends—those He invested most of His time in. With the mishmash gospel being preached today, and with the current view of Jesus acting like some 1960s flower child hippie who walked around saying, "Peace and love," to everyone, the following points will be mind-blowing for most in the church who think Jesus acted like some equal opportunity spiritual guru who befriended and invested His time the same with everyone.

How Jesus Chose Friends

When most people think of how to choose their friends, they have more of a worldly, casual concept than a biblical one. In John 15:15 Jesus told His disciples that He considered them friends and not servants. Since the kingdom of God is based upon relationship and not ministry, it is important we know how to choose our friends wisely. Many churches and even Christians attempt to engender friendships merely to have nice fellowship together. However, true kingdom fellowship should be with the ultimate goal of getting closer to someone to advance kingdom purposes. Most folks are too quick to call someone a friend or choose friends just because they have a few things in common. Choosing friends should be a lot more important than just picking someone as a friend you only work with or enjoy watching a football game with. Merely liking someone should not be the only criteria for friendship.

There are many people I would like to consistently hang out with, but when it comes to the kingdom, there is more to it than that. I have to ask myself if I am called to build with someone before I make a long-term commitment. The reason is obvious: a person's destiny is often determined by those closest to him or her regarding quality time spent, mutual goals, and common purpose. You are whom you choose to hang with the most. The following are some of the criteria Jesus used to choose His friends.

Jesus prayed before choosing His friends.

In Luke 6:12–13 Jesus prayed all night before He chose the twelve people who would become closest to Him. This shows His choice of a friend was not haphazard; neither should ours be.

The friends of Jesus lived lives of obedience to God.

In John 15:14 Jesus said, "You are my friends if you do what I command you." It would be foolish for believers to make their closest friends and confidantes people who live purposeless lives before the Lord. This is not to say that we cannot have friends who do not follow Christ. Jesus at times spent time with sinners (Luke 7:34). However, He did not hang out with them merely to have a good time but to win them to His Father so that they could eventually live a life of obedience.

Also, these sinners were not the ones He invested the most time with unless they became His disciples. Paul encouraged Timothy to "pursue righteousness, faith, love, and peace, along with those who call on the Lord from a pure heart" (2 Tim. 2:22). Consequently we should not be close friends with someone unless he or she is serious about pursuing the things of God.

Jesus chose His friends to be with Him in order to send them out.

Mark 3:14 teaches that the primary expectation Jesus had at first with those He chose as friends was to spend time together. They had to learn to "do life" together, not just do Bible studies and attend synagogue. However, the ultimate result of their proximity to Him was to be sent out to preach. After all, how could they proclaim a Jesus they did not know, and how could they know Him unless they spent quality time with Him? No one should be quick to call someone a friend before he or she has spent much quality time with that person and knows him or her personally.

Jesus chose friends He could share His heart with.

John 15:15 teaches us that Jesus shared His heart with His friends who understood Him. In Matthew 13:11 Jesus told His friends, "To you it has been given to know the secrets of the kingdom of heaven, but to them [non-friends] it has not been given." If someone cannot understand your heart or believe in your vision, it will be difficult for that person to be a true kingdom friend.

Jesus proactively chose His friends.

In the context of how He chose friends, John 15:16 teaches us that people did not choose Him, but vice versa. Although this passage is also referring to salvation, it shows that His methodology for choosing friends was proactive (not reactive) based on their calling to build with Him. Consequently we should determine in our hearts who we should pursue in a friendship. Don't merely pick those who desire to be close to you; proactively choose people based on a leading of the Lord. Not everyone who wanted to be close to Jesus was given that access. Out of the multitudes He had an inner circle of only three, then twelve, and then seventy. The others only had access to Him during brief moments of their lives. If you are going to be fruitful in the kingdom, you cannot spend a lot of time with every person you meet. For example, I do not feel guilty for not answering every Facebook message or email sent to me. If I did, I would either suffer burnout, leave important work undone, or lose my primary focus and miss my calling.

Jesus' friends received His hard sayings.

In John 6:66–68 many of His disciples left Him because they could not receive the meat of the Word! His true friends were thus separated from those who were merely temporary acquaintances. Your true friends will stand by you even when God gives you a hard saying or a call to do something that is not understood by many other people.

Jesus' friends were those who stood by Him during His trials.

Luke 22:28–29 shows that His closest friends were those who stuck it out with Him during His earthly trials. God will often allow you to go through a severe personal or ministerial trial to test those around you to demonstrate who your real friends are. You can only build with those who are faithful to you during difficult times and not just when things are going well.

In conclusion, Jesus integrated His social need to have friends with His kingdom calling. He never separated the two, and neither should we. Hence, we should proactively choose our closest friends to be those whom God has called us to build His kingdom with. This doesn't mean we act like some cults that forbid their followers from socializing with so-called nonbelievers and from loving and serving their immediate family. Furthermore, we who are called to help unleash potential in other people have to prioritize our mentees so that the bulk of our time invested is with those who will bear the most fruit for the glory of God.

Chapter 11

The Power of Community

*O*NE OF THE most important things I have discovered in my study of Scripture is the fact that it was written with a Hebraic mindset. Before this I found out that much of the time, I was imposing my individualistic, American cultural perspective on biblical passages, which negated the proper way to interpret Scripture. As a result I would individualize a lot of the promises of Scripture and did not understand how Jesus, as a Jew, would never have conceived of attempting to unleash the potential in a follower apart from the faith community He was building.

My cultural imposition of American culture on the Bible is nothing new. It has been going on at least since the church moved away from the influence of Jerusalem toward the Roman/Greco Hellenistic mindset starting in the second century,[1] when much of the church embraced an individualistic interpretation of faith and life. Numerous parachurch organizations make the same mistake as they attempt to make disciples without the local church being front and center in their mission and methodology. They reason that since Jesus made twelve disciples who became apostles—before the church—they can imitate Him and make disciples "one on one" without local church participation.

What these organizations fail to realize is that Jesus always had the church in mind when He invested time in His disciples. For example, He told them in His final discourse that He would not leave them as orphans but would send the Holy Spirit, who would continue the ministry of Jesus through them. In the same way Jesus ministered by the power of the Holy Spirit, they too would minister through the Spirit (John 14:16–18). He even said to them, "When the Helper comes, whom I will send to you from the Father, that is the Spirit of truth who proceeds from the Father, He will testify about me, and you will testify also, because you have been with me from the beginning" (John 15:26–27, NASB). He said further to His disciples:

> But when He, the Spirit of truth, comes, He will guide you into all the truth; for He will not speak on His own initiative, but whatever He hears, He will speak; and He will disclose to you what is to come. He will glorify Me, for He will take of Mine and will disclose it to you. All things that the Father

has are Mine; therefore I said that He takes of Mine
and will disclose it to you.

—JOHN 16:13–15, NASB

Furthermore, we see in the beginning of the Acts narrative that the historian Luke connected the church to the ministry of Jesus when he opened his statement by saying that his Gospel (Luke's Gospel) was about "all that Jesus began to do and teach." (See Acts 1:1, NASB.) By saying that it recorded what Jesus "began to do and teach," he was framing the Acts narrative as a continuation of the ministry of Jesus through the church! That is to say, to have a discipleship model without the church in mind is a huge mistake. My own experience as a pastor has shown me that besides the preaching of the Word and worship, the primary way a person learns how to walk in his divine purpose is by serving in a local congregation. I have learned that the process of being made one with other brothers and sisters in the church is the key for learning how to love; forgive; be patient; empower the weak; use spiritual gifts; receive strength, hope and encouragement; and learn the primary ways God designed to use you. For instance, a person can say all he wants about being called to be a full-time church pastor. However, if the rest of the congregation does not hear or sense the voice of the shepherd in him, then that is a sign that he is not called to be a pastor.

When people ask me why they need to participate in a local church in order to be a follower of Jesus, I use worldly examples to make my point. I ask these people, "Can you learn how to play professional baseball, football, basket-ball, tennis, soccer, and hockey without joining a team?" Of course the answer is no!

The apostle Paul makes an even greater case for corporate involvement when he compares the church to a biological body. He says:

> For the body is not one member, but many. If the foot
> says, "Because I am not a hand, I am not a part of the
> body," it is not for this reason any the less a part of
> the body. And if the ear says, "Because I am not an
> eye, I am not a part of the body, " it is not for this
> reason any the less a part of the body. If the whole
> body were an eye, where would the hearing be? If the
> whole were hearing, where would the sense of smell
> be? But now God has placed the members, each one
> of them in the body, just as He desired. If they were
> all one member, where would the body be? But now
> there are many members but one body. And the eye
> cannot say to the hand, "I have no need of you"; or
> again the head to the feet, "I have no need of you."
> —1 CORINTHIANS 12:14–21, NASB

So when people ask me if they need a local church to follow Jesus, I tell them, "You can go to heaven without participating in a local church, but you cannot function properly without the church in the same way that if I cut off my finger, it can no longer function apart from being connected to the hand, which is connected to the wrist and the arm." In other words, one needs the other to function.

The Triune God Is Our Model for Community

Jesus made the most powerful case for participating in the body of Christ when He taught us in His high priestly prayer (John 17) that believers are called to be one with each other the same way the Father and Son are one with one another. That is to say, believers are called to function together in oneness in the same way the Father, Son, and Holy Spirit work together. The communion the triune God has is not just fellowship. It is purposeful oneness that resulted in the creation of the universe and in which the magnanimous plan of redemption unfolded in Christ.

Together let's zero in on one aspect of this prayer as recorded in the Gospel of John. Jesus prayed:

> I do not ask on behalf of these alone, but for those also who believe in Me through their word; that they may be one; even as You, Father, are in Me and I in you, that they also may be in Us, so that the world may believe that You sent Me. The glory which You have given Me I have given to them, that they may be one, just as We are one; I in them and You in Me, that they may be perfected in unity, so that the world may know that You sent Me, and loved them, even as You have loved Me. Father, I desire that they also, whom You have given Me, be with Me where I am, so that they may see My glory which You have given Me, for You loved Me before the foundation of the world.
>
> —JOHN 17:20–24, NASB

This powerful prayer by Jesus shows that the kind of unity God expects of His church is modeled by the unity between the Father and Son. This should obligate every Christ follower to have strong functional unity with brothers and sisters in the church. Jesus even said that the effectiveness of world evangelization depends upon the quality of functional unity or oneness the church walks in.[2]

Jesus then prayed that the church would have the same glory the Father gave the Son so that we would be one with one another and with the Father! This is quite amazing because when we think of the glory of God, we usually limit it to the cloud falling down in a meeting replete with people getting saved and healed. However, in this context Jesus is saying that another aspect of the glory of God is when God knits hearts and minds together as one in Him. Truly unity and oneness are so difficult for humanity that when people can come together in one heart and mind in Christ, it is an act of God!

Finally, Jesus says that we would be perfected in unity so that the world would know that Jesus was sent by the Father. This powerful phrase, *perfected in unity*, shows that it is impossible for a person to mature in Christ apart from walking in oneness with other members of the church. The word *perfect* here is not referring to sinless perfection but to maturity; hence, Jesus is saying here that the process of having unity with other members of the body of Christ—which often includes having to walk in forgiveness and kindness, serving one another, empowering one another, bearing with one another's faults and weaknesses, and so on—is the only process that can work to mature us as Christ followers.

Consequently it's much easier to be a strong Christian reading the Bible and praying alone in your room than it is to learn how to walk out your faith in the context of people in which you may have ethnic, cultural, personality, and value differences, and in which there may be a clash of egos and ambition, along with the projection of the false self disguised as religious performance. Jesus is saying if you can learn to walk in oneness with His people, then that is the proof that the glory of God is working in you to mature you and make you Christlike!

Jesus did not work individually with each disciple but put them all in the cauldron of intense team ministry in the context of self-focused crowds vying for their attention and help. He put twelve men together with various economic and vocational backgrounds, along with various intents and agendas of the heart. It was not easy ministering together as a team, even with Jesus functioning as their leader. For example, whenever I think I am having a bad day, all I have to do is turn to the portion of Scripture showing what happened the last evening of Jesus' life leading up to His crucifixion. We find in the Luke narrative that the same evening Jesus shared His last supper with His twelve, all of the following took place:

- One of the twelve betrayed Jesus (Luke 22:21).

- The rest of the twelve were arguing amongst each other regarding which of them was the greatest in God's kingdom (Luke 22:24–27).

- Satan tried to get Peter—the leader of the burgeoning Christ movement—to fall away from the faith (Luke 22:31, 34).

- His three closest disciples all fell asleep from sorrow and depression and could not even pray with Jesus in His darkest hour (Luke 22:44–46).

- One of the twelve led an army of antagonists that arrested Jesus and led Him to His eventual death (Luke 22:47–53).

In conclusion, it is clear that if we want to release potential in people, we need to eventually get them to serve God in the context of a local congregation. Jesus taught His disciples to fulfill the will of God by learning to work together as a team rather than as individuals. It was these kind of life experiences they lived through together that would prepare them for the much harder tests and trials that awaited them once the church they were to lead was born soon thereafter on the day of Pentecost (Acts 2).

Chapter 12

The Power of Secure Leadership

*O*VER THE YEARS, I have observed the fact that the more insecure a person is, the less willing and able he or she is to unleash high-end potential in others. Conversely the more secure a person is, the more willing and able that person is to recognize and release great potential in others. If a person feels small inside, the person will think everyone is a giant trying to kill him or her. When our interior self is strong, we feel comfortable around others, enabling us to operate at high capacity. One of the things that made Jesus the greatest releaser of potential who ever lived was the fact that He was very secure in Himself. He never walked around uptight trying to prove Himself to other people.

One encounter He had with the religious leaders who opposed Him highlights His internal security as a person:

Then Jesus again spoke to them saying, "I am the Light of the world; he who follows Me will not walk in the darkness, but will have the Light of life." So the Pharisees said to Him, "You are testifying about Yourself; Your testimony is not true." Jesus answered and said to them, "Even if I testify about Myself, My testimony is true, for I know where I came from and where I am going; but you do not know where I come from or where I am going. You judge according to the flesh; I am not judging anyone. But even if I do judge, My judgment is true; for I am not alone in it, but I and the Father who sent Me."

—JOHN 8:12–16, NASB

In this encounter it is evident that Jesus did not need affirmation from other men because He already had the affirmation of His Father. Notice that He had no problem declaring the truth about Himself when He said that He was the light of the world. This is because secure people can speak honestly about themselves without succumbing to false humility or pride. Jesus intimated that the confidence and strength He had to testify about Himself came from the fact that He knew where He came from and where He was going. That is to say, He was grounded and established in His root identity, which ensured that He had a fixed path ahead given to Him by His Father so that no human would be able to hinder His desired future from taking place.

That being said, one of the calls we have to be Christlike is to be secure in Him the way He was secure in His Father.

The more secure we are in Christ, the more we can help secure and establish others in the faith and in their ability to unleash their potential. This is because the more secure in Christ we are, the more discernment we will have to recognize the potential in others without getting threatened or insecure because of it. The more secure we are in Christ, the more we can help others become secure in Him so they too can continue the cycle of helping ground others in Christ. After all, the deeper the roots of a tree, the higher the tree can grow. The heights we can reach in Christ are determined by the depths of our roots in Christ. The less rooted in Christ we are, the less rooted in Christ our disciples will be.

The following are some of the traits of secure people:

- Secure people are not afraid of high-end potential in other people.

- Secure people are not afraid to help other people accomplish greater works than they, themselves, have accomplished.

- Secure people are able to keep proper boundaries because they are centered people who are not running around ignoring personal and family boundaries or trying to create opportunity to elevate themselves.

- Secure people have more wisdom to impart to others because when you are secure, you are more still before the Lord and less anxious, which makes it easier for you to discern the will of God for yourself and others.

- Secure people are able to impart faith and balance into other people.

- Secure people leave room for others to shine. The more secure a person is, the easier it is for him or her to genuinely celebrate the successes of other people. Insecure people crave constant attention and suck the air out of every room they walk into. They long to be the bride at every wedding and the corpse at every funeral. They can't bear it when someone or something else besides themselves is the center of attention.

- Secure people live to prepare other people to carry on their legacy. They are people who strive to work themselves out of a job and rejoice when another person can do a job as good or better than they can.

It goes without saying that the more insecure a person is, the less likely the person will be successful in pouring into other people and helping them unleash potential. These are some of the traits of insecure people:

- Insecure people feel threatened by other, stronger, gifted individuals. Instead of pouring the fire of God into others, they attempt to pour cold water over others to quench their zeal and passion for God.

- Insecure people rarely delegate and often micromanage others.

- Insecure people rarely attract other people with high upside in potential.

- Insecure people surround themselves with yes men and women because they feel threatened by those who think for themselves.

- Insecure people rarely celebrate the success of other people.

- Insecure people focus on releasing their own potential more than the potential of others.

- Insecure people are only team players when they are in charge.

- Insecure people are only behind an endeavor when they are leading it and get the credit for it.

- Insecure people are driven for success more than they are led by the Holy Spirit.

- Insecure people are usually uncomfortable in intimate, social settings.

- Insecure people become the bottleneck of whatever mission they are participating in.

As we close this chapter, I cannot overstate the importance for those desiring to unleash potential in others to make sure they, themselves, are attempting to find their security, fulfillment, and identity in the Lord Jesus. If not, they will always limit both their effectiveness and the effectiveness of those around them.

Understanding Your Purpose to Unleash Potential in Others

Jesus knew His mission and articulated it before He ministered in a new city. We find an example of this in the Luke narrative where Jesus preached for the first time in His hometown of Nazareth. In the synagogue He opened the scroll of the prophet Isaiah and read from it these words:

> The Spirit of the Lord is upon me, because he has anointed me to proclaim good news to the poor. He has sent me to proclaim liberty to the captives and recovering of sight to the blind, to set at liberty those who are oppressed.
>
> —LUKE 4:18–19

Jesus knew where He came from and where He was headed in the future. (See John 8:14.) He had both short-term and long-term goals, as we can see from Scripture. "And he said to them, 'Go and tell that fox, "Behold, I cast out demons and perform cures today and tomorrow, and

146

the third day I finish my course"'" (Luke 13:32). What sustained Jesus on the cross was "the joy that was set before him" (Heb. 12:2). He also understood and articulated the primary purpose He had for coming into the world, which came out in a conversation with Pilate during His trial before His subsequent crucifixion. "And Pilate asked him, 'Are you the King of the Jews?' And he answered him, 'You have said so'" (Luke 23:3).

In light of this, I noticed that Jesus was never in a rush as He walked among us, often taking time to minister to someone while He was on His way to minister to someone else (Mark 5:21–43). This is foreign to many of us who attempt time-management methodologies instead of utilizing life-management principles in which each day centers around a major agenda or category instead of needing to map out each minute of the day. The more focused a person is, the less rushed and harried he or she is. This is because focus lessens the chance the person will engage in unnecessary activity that eats up time. The general rule of thumb is the more unfocused activity a person is involved in, the less productivity, profit, and time he or she will have for self-renewal, family, and meaningful ministry. Hence, the more unfocused a person is, the less effective he or she will be in helping unleash potential in other people.

If we are going to help people go from living ordinary to extraordinary lives, we need to learn from Jesus and be purposeful as He was. If we are going to pour our lives into others, then we cannot live our lives chaotically, always in a rush. The more intentional we are, the more purposeful our lives will be, the less of a rush we will be in, and the more time we will have to pour into and mentor others.

Let us close this chapter with a summary of the power principles of Jesus that made Him a master teacher and mentor.

Jesus knew His purpose.

In John 18:37 Jesus told Pilate that He was the King: "Then Pilate said to him, 'So you are a king?' Jesus answered, 'You say that I am a king. For this purpose I was born and for this purpose I have come into the world—to bear witness to the truth. Everyone who is of the truth listens to my voice.'"

There was nothing ambiguous about Jesus. He knew the *what* and the *why* regarding His birth and purpose on the earth.

Jesus knew His mission.

Luke 4:18–19 illustrates that Jesus had a vision regarding what He was supposed to do in ministry to fulfill His mission.

Jesus had specific goals.

Luke 13:31–33 shows that Jesus had a goal of where and when He was going to be in His travels.

Jesus spent much time daily in prayer and only did what He saw His Father do.

This principle is clearly illustrated in Isaiah 50:4–7 and John 5:18–19.

Harald Bredesen once said to a group of pastors: "If ministers would concentrate on only doing that which pleases the Lord and put that first, then everyone they are supposed to please will be pleased and ministers would not suffer burnout."

Jesus focused on people, not programs.

Matthew 9:36 shows us that Jesus was cognizant of people and felt compassion for them. In Matthew 23:2–4 Jesus teaches against putting heavy burdens on people without helping them. Also in Matthew 23:23 Jesus put down leaders who emphasized the tithe without also emphasizing justice and mercy for people.

Jesus concentrated on catching men and on leadership development instead of administrative duties.

Jesus only focused on what He and His twelve (and later on His seventy) could accomplish. He wasn't bogged down with a lot of administration because He delegated to His disciples everything needed to release Him to concentrate on preaching, teaching, and discipling.

Most churches would prosper if they would attempt to do away with every ministry that doesn't focus on evangelism and making disciples.

Jesus knew where He came from and where He was going.

In John 8:14 Jesus told the Jews that His testimony was true because He knew where He came from and where He was going.

If people don't know where they came from (the genesis of life reveals the purpose and journey of life), then how are they going to know why they are here and where they are supposed to go?

Jesus wasn't ego driven; He was moved by compassion to minister (Mark 1:41-44).

Leaders who are driven instead of being led of the Lord are often competitive, insecure, and egocentric regarding their ministry. They may work hard, but their low self-esteem drives them hard in their search for significance.

Jesus knew when His ministry would be finished.

John 19:30 shows that Jesus knew when His ministry was over and said, "It is finished," before He gave up His spirit and died. Many people don't end well, don't finish their purpose, or stay at a position long after they should have handed it off to a younger or more gifted leader to adequately accomplish the corporate mission.

Jesus didn't minister outside of His assignment.

Mark 7:27 shows that Jesus wasn't going to minister to the Syrophoenician woman because she wasn't under the covenant with God and didn't fit His target audience. Furthermore, He instructed His disciples not to go to any of the gentiles or Samaritans; He wanted them to stay focused and purposeful (Matt. 10:5-6). When you go outside of your God-given assignment, you step out of His grace and favor and minister out of the flesh. This leads to ministerial burnout.

We can't be everyone's savior. We are not everyone's answer to prayer. You are not called to help every person you meet. Sometimes Satan will even send people your way to wear you out! Stay within your assignment, and you will prosper and be satisfied.

In our church I refuse to start a ministry, even if there is a great need, until God gives me a leader qualified to oversee it. The reason for this is if I don't have a leader to manage a ministry, then either my office staff or I will have to manage the new ministry, which will put undue stress on us.

Jesus didn't waste His time in meaningless conversation.

John 12:20–23 records how Jesus never honored the request of the Greeks, who wanted to see Him, but ignored them and continued to enter the next phase of His ministry. I am not obligated to return everyone's phone call or email, or meet with every person who wants to meet with me. I can't satisfy everyone's agenda for my life. I am only obligated to please the Lord and do what I see my Father command me to do.

Jesus operated out of His inner circle and delegated to them the ministry of helps that released Him to focus on preaching, teaching, praying, and accomplishing His purpose.

Jesus had His three, His twelve, and His seventy minister to Him and for Him. The Gospel accounts show that it was His disciples who shopped for food (John 4:8), which released Him to minister to Samaria. Also, it was His disciples who arranged for the multitudes to sit down so He could feed them (John 6:10). Peter and John were told to prepare the Upper Room for Jesus to conduct the famous last supper (Luke 22:8–13). Jesus was asleep on a boat while His disciples took Him to His next destination (Mark 4:35–41).

In conclusion, if we are going to be effective mentors who unleash potential in others, we must live purposeful lives that give us the capacity to focus and flourish so that we can release others to their destiny and calling.

Chapter 13

Understanding Struggle

JESUS WENT TO the cross before He was resurrected; He experienced great pain before He was raised to life in power. Ultimately His pain was our gain. In order to be like Jesus, we too have to learn how to allow pain (not for our redemption) to shape us so that we can walk in the humility and wisdom of Jesus and become wounded healers as He was (Isa. 53:4–6).

In my almost forty years as a Christian leader I have noticed that most of my emotional and spiritual growth has come during times of intense pain and challenges to my leadership. While most of us would love to grow merely from the accumulation of information, the truth is that we need to experience illumination in order for the knowledge to transform our inner being. That is why I often tell people, "We cannot grow from only attending Bible studies and saying prayers; we must live these studies and prayers out in our lives so we can realize the growth!"

There is a growing trend in academia to combine practice with knowledge, since practitioners have more knowledge of their subjects than those who only view data all day on computers. Practitioner research produces the only kind of data we can trust. This is similar to how generals and armies can only become adroit and gain true battle skill by being engaged in actual combat. Medical doctors will never learn only by taking classes; they must practice on real people in order to be proficient. I would never want to be the first patient a medical doctor ever operates upon to gain skill. This is why doctors will never tell their patients what kind of real experience they have until they have a good track record of actual patient practice.

Regarding pain, there is something about the human brain, specifically the feeling of pain and pleasure that connects these experiences to cause us to choose certain behavior patterns. When I was a child and touched a burning stove, I learned from that painful experience never to do that again! No matter how many times my parents told me not to do that, I had to learn the hard way.

As a Christ follower I have learned that when I put the kingdom of God first in my life, all the things I need are supernaturally given to me. But when I put my fleshly desires first, things do not go well, and I pay the consequences. These negative experiences are for the purpose of aiding me in my spiritual growth. Sometimes God allows painful experiences to take place in our lives even if we did not do anything wrong because He knows it is part of the preparation to get us to the next level. The human heart is deceitfully wicked and desperately sick (Jer. 17:9) because of our sinful nature. Unfortunately the only way we sinful humans will walk in brokenness and humility is through learning by suffering in our flesh (Dan. 11:35).

I have rarely met a young minister who didn't think he was ready to be a great leader with a great title. But I have met quite a few older, wiser ministers who have learned to die to the goal of achieving great ministry celebrity status because they have learned through pain how truly fleeting all those things the world regards as successful are. A biblical case in point is found in King David. David was anointed king of Israel in 1 Samuel 16, but he wasn't actually given the title and function until more than a decade later, after King Saul died. (In 2 Samuel 2 David was anointed king of Judah, and in chapter 5 he was anointed king over all Israel.) David had the gifts, abilities, and anointing to be king when he was seventeen years old, but it wasn't until he had suffered pain for thirteen years due to the persecution of a flesh-driven, egocentric king that he was emotionally ready to ascend the throne.

Oftentimes young people are frustrated in life because they think they have the ability to stand in a certain position that someone else above them has. But these young people do not understand that because of our sinful nature, God has to use the school of pain to prepare us for promotion. I don't believe God has ever promoted me when I thought I was ready. Thank God He waited until He knew I was ready for more responsibility.

God loved David so much that He didn't want him to be a king until he had every semblance of fleshly control processed out of him. It has been my experience that before God promotes me to the next level, I am already walking in that higher-level anointing and authority but without the position and the title. I may have the anointing first, but then comes a series of challenging tests meant to compel me to beat the flesh into subjection, so I don't explode with pride when I get to the next level. The transition has to take place internally before it manifests externally.

Before a woman gives birth, she has a beautiful baby living inside of her for nine months. Not only that, but right before the baby is born, the greatest trauma to the mother takes place while she is pushing that baby out! Many believers quit while on the delivery table; the pain causes them to give up before what they are birthing has had a chance to be fully formed and pushed through. May God help us to fully push through the pain until promotion comes.

One day I was pondering that all the leaders I know with much influence seem to have one thing in common: they have all suffered much in their lives. In fact, every one of them has a particular cross to bear, or he has gone through horrendous seasons of pain and suffering that were part of a divine process that made him and continues to mold him into the highly effective leader he is today. These challenges can be relational issues with a spouse, children, other leaders, and so on, or they can be personal issues related to his spiritual, emotional, or physical well-being. We see this illustrated in Acts when God tells Ananias that Paul will have to suffer much for the name of Jesus. (See Acts 9:16.) We can read Paul's own testimony about himself regarding the reason for his suffering in 2 Corinthians:

> I must go on boasting. Though there is nothing to be gained by it, I will go on to visions and revelations of the Lord. I know a man in Christ who fourteen years ago was caught up to the third heaven—whether in the body or out of the body I do not know, God knows. And I know that this man was caught up into paradise—whether in the body or out of the body I do not know, God knows—and he heard things that cannot be told, which man may not utter. On behalf of this man I will boast, but on my own behalf I will not boast, except of my weaknesses—though if I should wish to boast, I would not be a fool, for I would be speaking the truth; but I refrain from it, so that no one may think more of me than he sees in me or hears from me. So to keep me from becoming conceited because of the surpassing greatness of the revelations, a thorn was given me in the flesh, a messenger of Satan to harass me, to keep me from becoming conceited. Three times I pleaded with the Lord about this, that it should leave me. But he said to me, "My grace is sufficient for you, for my power is made perfect in weakness." Therefore I will boast all the more gladly of my weaknesses, so that the power of Christ may rest upon me. For the sake of Christ, then, I am content with weaknesses,

insults, hardships, persecutions, and calamities. For
when I am weak, then I am strong.

—2 CORINTHIANS 12:1–10

According to this passage, Paul's suffering was connected to his leadership ability and great calling, which
had to be tempered through his suffering because of our
human sin nature that has a propensity to boast about our
own accomplishments. God has to allow pain in our lives
to keep us dependent upon Him because all of us are born
in sin with the fleshly tendencies to brag about our own
accomplishments and trust in our own gifts, abilities, and
flesh instead of in His grace. As I view my own life and
the lives of others I know personally, I can see how the
very things that make us successful are also connected to
our sin nature, which has been the root of much sin in
our lives. For example, in my own life the stubbornness,
perseverance, and tendency to move forward for the sake
of Christ in spite of all obstacles is connected to how in
my childhood I coped with rejection, isolation, and pain
through making a name for myself by excelling in street
fighting, sports, and music, and in other areas of life. This
was all in an effort to carve out a name and identity for
myself so I would be praised, respected, and celebrated by
my peers. Although this developed in me qualities of perseverance in the midst of pain and suffering, it was for my
glory and not for God's glory!

Thus, the development of qualities I use to this day
are part of my leadership portfolio. My gifts and abilities

are directly connected to the habits and patterns I developed out of my sin nature and my desire to carve out a name for myself for the sake of self-worth and self-esteem. This shows me that God even used my sins for His glory. Consequently the gifts and abilities I use today as a leader in the body of Christ were originally inspired, molded, and developed in the fiery furnace of self-survival in my childhood. My gifts and calling are inextricably connected to the very sin nature Jesus had to die for! This is why God has to continually allow great challenges, pain, and suffering in my life as a way of tempering my tendency to depend upon myself, honor myself, and trust in myself for results.

The greater the leaders, the more stubborn they have to be to resist temptation, to stay focused, and to be successful, even though this same stubbornness may have originally developed and emanated out of their personal rebellion against God before they were saved. Thus, there is always a fine line between our great leadership qualities and our sinful tendencies to rebel against God and build our own kingdoms. This also explains why great leaders often fall into scandal, especially if they allow their hectic schedules to crowd out their continual need for spiritual formation in God's presence.

Going back to the apostle Paul, as he matured, he actually bragged more about his weaknesses than his accomplishments so the power of Christ could rest on him. What a far cry from some of today's preachers who are constantly bragging about how much victory, power, and accomplishments they have in their ministries. In reality the more spiritually immature leaders are, the more they will brag about accomplishments. The more mature they are, the more they will brag about their weaknesses and glorify Christ's grace that empowers them. Understanding these concepts should help us in two areas. First, instead of discouraging Christ followers, this should be a great source of encouragement. Many believers suffer silently because they are embarrassed and think they are the only ones continually dealing with painful issues. Satan will use this to cause a person to quit out of sheer discouragement and a sense of failure. We should take heart and know that we are not alone in our pain. To the extent people have influence, they will have to endure the process of pain so their gifts and abilities can be continually redeemed for the glory and honor of God.

The key to discovering and dealing with the dominant sin issues in our lives is to honestly reflect on our talents, gifts, and abilities and how we have trusted in them to manipulate others, control our environments for self-autonomy, and carve out a name for ourselves. This is like how Lucifer attempted to do the same when his pride motivated him to attempt to exalt himself above the throne of God for self-autonomy and self-glorification (Isa. 14:12–14). Understanding this enables us to have greater insight and appreciation for the depths and riches of the love and grace of God, who will use the very abilities that are connected to our self-glorification and fleshly preservation to shape and form us for His purposes. God surrounds power with problems so that by the time we have power and influence, we have become so broken, humble, and dependent upon God that we would not be so quick to share the glory with God for the great accomplishments that arise out of our feeble efforts.

The Believer and Spiritual Warfare

There are some believers who falsely believe that if they have a lot of faith, they will not undergo any suffering, severe tests, or satanic attacks. Nothing could be further from the truth! Actually, the opposite is true. For example, in the Book of Job, chapters 1 and 2, God actually asks Satan if he considered His servant Job. Hence, God brought Job to Satan's attention, not because Job was in sin, but because Job was the greatest servant of God on the earth at that time (Job 1:6–12; 2:3–6).

There are other examples in Scripture. Acts 19:15 illustrates how Paul the apostle was known not only in heaven but also in hell! He had their attention! This is why Paul states that he begged the Lord to take away the messenger of Satan that followed him around (2 Cor. 12:1–8). This messenger was not sickness but harassment, as we see from reading the context in 2 Corinthians 11:17–34. First Peter 5:8–9 teaches that Satan roams the earth seeking someone to devour, which also goes along with the Job narrative (Job 1:7). When we read the context of all these passages, especially in regard to the satanic focus on both Paul and Job, we can come to the conclusion that the devil's main focus is to thwart, divert, distract, and disarm the servants of God who are promoting the rule of God on the earth as it is in heaven. Heaven is the only realm in the universe where everything is perfectly aligned under King Jesus because the devil was displaced from heaven (Rev. 12:7–12). Consequently when someone on earth wants to bring the influence of the kingdom of God on earth as it is in heaven, Satan erupts with fear and anger against that person since he doesn't want to be thrown out of another place!

This is why it seems as though a person following the will of God will sometimes have the most difficult tests, trials, and resistance, as opposed to some saints who are casual seekers of God. Satan is no dummy. Why should he attack a Christian who is a bad example to others and who is already deceived and in his grip? He will focus the most on those who are the biggest threats to his desire to perform a power grab from God over the earth realm! Remember, God gave Adam a commission to have His rule over the whole earth (Gen. 1:28), and immediately after that the devil came and convinced both Adam and Eve to disobey God and abandon their posts as God's vice regents over the earth (Gen. 3:1–8).

Since that time Satan has been jealously attempting to protect his control over the earthly realm he stole through subverting Adam, including its systems of government, commerce, media, the arts, science, and education. Those who attempt to bring God's influence in these realms will most likely experience some of the highest levels of satanic resistance. The apostle Paul had a messenger from Satan follow him everywhere he went that caused riots and persecutions (2 Cor. 12:1–8), only because he was turning the present world system upside down (Acts 17).

So if you are sold out for God, don't be discouraged when you are attacked or allow yourself to be deceived into thinking that the only reason you are in intense spiritual warfare or tribulation is because you may have missed God. It may be the opposite. You are being targeted because you are hitting the divine bull's-eye! This is why Paul admonished believers to stand strong in the Lord: "For our struggle is not against flesh and blood, but against the rulers, against the authorities, against the powers of this dark world and against the spiritual forces of evil in the heavenly realms" (Eph. 6:10–13, NIV). Notice Paul said "our struggle," meaning he was including himself in this struggle. Every time there was an open door for ministry, he had many adversaries. This is a biblical principle (1 Cor. 16:9).

Do not ever think that just because God is calling you to do something, it will be easy. Jesus did the will of God, and He was crucified. Church history tells us Paul was beheaded. It's not how many years we live but what we do with the years we live that matters! So what do we do when we are in a time of spiritual warfare that Paul calls "the day of evil" in Ephesians 6:13 (NIV)? Paul tells us in this passage to be strong in the Lord and to stand firm; in other words, do not quit (vv. 10–13). The apostle Peter also tells us to resist the devil, standing firm in the faith (1 Pet. 5:9). Peter knows firsthand that faith in God is the key to standing firm in the midst of the day of evil because when he denied

Christ three times, Jesus prayed for him that his "faith" would not fail (Luke 22:31–32). Therefore, do not be afraid when you are in tribulation because Jesus has already overcome the world (John 16:33)!

All Christ followers, especially those endeavoring to unleash potential in others, will be resisted and even attacked by the enemy of our souls. However, I want to reinforce the importance for Christian mentors to have endurance and the proper attitude toward pain and suffering, especially the kind of pain that is both emotional and psychological.

Pain to Prosper You

Pain is unavoidable in this world. Again, the primary kind of pain I am referring to is emotional, mental, and psychological pain. Jesus promised us that in the world we will suffer tribulation (John 16:33), which includes both physical and emotional in this context. There are many different reasons for pain. Some pain is self-inflicted, some is caused by unexpected tragedies such as an accident, some is caused by the behavior of other people, some is from mental and emotional trauma, some, like in the Book of Job, is from divine tests, and the list goes on. Irrespective of the cause, all pain has one thing in common: the redemptive potential to make an individual better or a family or team of leaders a better functioning community.

Nobody wants pain, and most people attempt to avoid it or run from it. Despite this, pain is indispensable for the purpose of God to be realized on earth. It is also indispensable for the unleashing of potential in our lives. Many who attempt to avoid pain try to medicate themselves with much activity, the pursuit of numerous relationships, or the abuse of substances such as drugs and alcohol. I too would rather avoid it, but when I am experiencing intense pain, it causes me to ponder its root causes, which causes me to become more self-aware. Since pain is the common experience of every human being, pain can brand us with an acute sense of empathy for fellow humans who are suffering through situations similar to what we have experienced (2 Cor. 1:3–7). A mere intellectual understanding of the Bible cannot accomplish this.

Pain can motivate us to go deeper in our key relationships and have less motivation for superficial ones. It can cause us to seek the Lord like never before to become more Christlike and endure suffering with His power and strength (Phil. 4:13). Pain can motivate us to prioritize our time and energy so that we become more focused on fulfilling our divine purpose in life. It can motivate us to get into the mental and emotional universe of others so that we can experience a fusion of horizons that enhance our key relationships. Pain motivates us to do things better the next time so we don't experience the same pain again. Through pain we learn patience, obedience, endurance, and the faithfulness of God in the midst of our suffering. Pain teaches us humility so that we can become grateful for the smallest things in life and loathe self-promotion. Pain leads us to discover that perhaps the greatest blessing in the world is not possessions, titles, or fame but inner peace, contentment, and the joy of the Lord. Through pain we can learn the leading of the Lord, the character and mind of God, and the meekness and gentleness of Christ (Ps. 32:8–9; 2 Cor. 10:1).

Through processing pain in the power of the Holy Spirit, we increase our spiritual and emotional capacity for pain, which in turn increases our leadership capacity. Samuel Chand's book *Leadership Pain* shows how a person's threshold for pain determines his or her capacity for influence.[1]

Pain helps you realize what is worth suffering for and the people and things you value most in life. You will not be willing to suffer for the people and entities you have no passion for, which is why some of our relationships don't last very long.

Pain causes us to focus on our main calling in life, which alone can motivate us to keep on keeping on (Heb. 12:1–2). It can make us bitter or better, enable us to learn godly conflict or run from it, cause us to blame others or grow internally, become a victim or experience a victory, be an overcomer or a complainer. God allowed the children of Israel to experience war to test them and teach them warfare (Judg. 3:1–4). Revelation 2–3 teaches the church that only the overcomers will inherit the blessings of God. Overcoming implies great challenge and its accompanying pain.

It is never our circumstances in life that destroy us; it's our response to circumstances that determines our trajectory. God expects us to overcome and continue in His kingdom purpose despite the immanent reality of intense pain and tribulation. (See Revelation 1:9.) Jesus, the greatest man who ever lived, was described as the suffering servant in Isaiah 53—"a man of sorrows and acquainted with grief" (v. 3). He was betrayed by someone close to Him (Judas) and forsaken by all of His followers, left alone to suffer on the cross. Note that the cross came before the resurrection! Jesus learned obedience through what He suffered (Heb. 5:8) and was made a faithful and great High Priest who can intercede for us because of the sufferings and tests He endured (Heb. 4:15–16). So if you are experiencing great pain, you have great company! The Lord Jesus Christ went before you and has already experienced more pain than any of us will ever experience, hopefully, which means He knows how to uphold us in His mighty hands. (See Isaiah 41:10; 43:2, 4.) Finally, the greatest call any of us will ever have is to be conformed to the image of Jesus Christ, which also involves fellowshipping in His sufferings (Phil. 3:10; Rom. 8:29–30). May we all grow into His image and have the same mind of Christ that Jesus had, as found in Philippians 2:4–11!

Pain to Prosper Others

When it comes to unleashing potential in others, we have to learn from Jesus that some of the greatest opportunities we will ever have to bond with others and develop their potential is to share with them our own painful journey. If they think that we never suffer, then those you mentor will not be able to relate to you. As we examine the Gospels, we see that Jesus exposed His disciples to conflict and shared

His pain. This is illustrated in the narratives related to the last supper and the experience of Jesus in the Garden of Gethsemane, as well as in His passion leading to the cross.

He told His disciples that if they were to stay with Him during His trials, afterward He would confer upon them a kingdom (Luke 22:28–30). Hence, part of the development of His disciples that unleashed their potential was to make them acutely aware of the reality of pain necessary to propagate the kingdom of God. Even St. Paul said that we must go through much tribulation to enter the kingdom of God (Acts 14:22). As one who has discipled people for almost four decades, I will tell you that one of the most powerful moments I have with my men is when I share my pain with them. Whether it is personal pain or ministerial pain, it is still effective.

My willingness to be vulnerable reveals a level of trust with my men that creates a powerful bond that cannot easily be broken. It also enables me to train and equip them as they see how I respond to my own painful experiences, and it enables them to understand my humanity as a person so that they do not lift me up on a pedestal in their own hearts and minds. Although the enemy attempts to use pain to destroy me, God uses it for His glory to unleash faith, hope, and potential in other people to advance His kingdom and for His glory.

Chapter 14

Understanding the Future

$\mathcal{S}$ome of the things that attracted followers to Jesus were the fact that He understood the times in which He lived, He stood against falsehood, and He gave clear guidance regarding the way forward. In other words, Jesus had prescience, not just presence. He understood the new thing God was ushering in, and at the same time, He knew that there were old wineskins that had to be forsaken. Jesus understood and gave honor to John the Baptist. Yet He also understood that John represented the law and the prophets, not the new covenant He was ushering in (Matt. 11:7–14). Jesus honored the past, yet at the same time, He did not get stuck in it and thereby limit the future. Scripture illustrates how Jesus understood the future.

- Jesus knew He was going to be crucified and prepared His disciples for this traumatic event (Mark 8:31–34).

- Jesus predicted He would rise again (Mark 8:31).

- Jesus knew He would die in Jerusalem (Luke 13:33).

- Jesus knew ahead of time that Satan was going to tempt Peter (Luke 22:31–34).

- Jesus knew who would betray Him (John 13:21–26).

- Jesus knew the Holy Spirit would take His place after His ascension and empower His disciples (John 14–16).

- His disciples believed He knew all things that were about to take place (John 16:30).

- Jesus knew how Peter, the emerging leader of the movement, was going to die (John 21:18–19).

In general, Jesus kept His disciples abreast of what was about to happen so that they would believe in Him (John 14:29). Of course nobody expects a mentor to know everything that is about to happen the way Jesus did, but all effective leaders have a general sense of where God is leading, current trends, and what God wants to accomplish in the future.

Also, Jesus promised His followers that one of the functions of the Holy Spirit is to show them things to come (John 16:13). Thus, we should expect the Lord to reveal to us pertinent things so that we can stay ahead of the curve and prepare His people for things to come. Scripture teaches us that a prudent person foresees the evil and hides himself, but the fool continues ahead and suffers the consequences (Prov. 22:3). Therefore, God expects a kind of prescience from all of his followers. Otherwise, how can we walk in wisdom and plan ahead?

When it comes to empowering and unleashing potential in others, we also need to function like the Sons of Issachar who were men who understood the times (the culture and current events of their day) and knew what to do about it (1 Chron. 12:32). The more leadership capacity you see in someone you are mentoring, the more responsibility you have to understand the times in which we live—not just the chronological times but the *kairos* moments, or divine times and seasons God is orchestrating upon the earth— so that you can pour it into those called to influence their communities and beyond. If we do not understand the current geopolitical, economic, and cultural trends, how can we pour into high-capacity leaders and help them release their potential?

However, even if we are mentoring a person to be a good father, good mother, or good worker (and not a high-capacity influencer), we are still responsible to help prepare that person for what is happening in society as well as helping him or her discern the will of God for his or her own future. To the extent that we prepare for and articulate the future, to that extent will those we are mentoring and influencing trust our judgment and our practical knowledge of God's working in the earth today.

During my years of pouring into men, I have been able to hear from God for many of them and warn them of traps they were about to walk into or even tell them what was going on in their lives, even though they never told anybody about it. This gave me incredible leverage with them because they knew that I cared enough about them to go to the throne room and have God speak to me for them and their families. Of course people don't always listen to their mentors. I have warned people in the spirit about geographic moves (even though I knew nothing about it in the natural), relationships they were getting into, and business ventures they were pursing. In most cases, when someone has already made up his mind, he will not listen to his mentor even though he knows God spoke to him through said mentor. In most (if not all) of these instances, failure to heed the warning word from the Lord resulted in disaster.

I am careful not to lord it over anyone's personal life, and I rarely give prophetic words dealing with the direction of a person's life. However, at times God will drop something in my spirit for a person, and I will deliver the word, whether it is an easy word or not. In most cases, the person will respect me for giving the word even if he does not ultimately align with it. Often when someone doesn't want to hear a hard word, I just pray for him and ask God to deal with his heart, trusting that he will come around before any permanent damage is done.

The point of all this is the fact that when we are entrusted by God to mentor and unleash potential in others, part of our responsibility is to have a sensitivity to the heart and mind of God for that person. This is how Jesus functioned with His disciples. The foreknowledge He had that Satan was desiring to sift Peter like wheat put Jesus ahead of the curve, allowing Him to pray for Peter. Jesus' prayers restored Peter back to faith in Him. As a result Peter became the first spokesperson and leader of the early church (Luke 22:31–34). When we are responsible to nurture and equip people, God is going to hold us responsible to hear from Him for them so that we will know how, when, and where to place them as well as to warn them of things to come so they can prepare and escape the snares the enemy sets up for them.

Chapter 15

Understanding
Spiritual Authority

ONE OF THE most striking things people discover when
they read about the life of Christ as found in the Gospels is the way Jesus submitted His every word, thought,
and action to the Father. This is even more amazing given
the fact that Jesus is Himself part of the triune Godhead
and as such is incredibly gifted, intelligent, and powerful;
hence, He does not seem like the prototypical person who
needs oversight. Yet even a quick glance through the Gospels shows how utterly dependent He was on the Father
and how obedient He was to Him. Jesus' words from
John's Gospel illustrates this:

> Jesus cried out and said, "He who believes in Me, does
> not believe in Me but in Him who sent Me. He who

sees me sees the One who sent Me....For I did not speak on My own initiative, but the Father Himself who sent Me has given Me a commandment as to what to say and what to speak. I know that His commandment is eternal life; therefore the things I speak, I speak just as the Father has told Me."

—JOHN 12:44–45, 49–50, NASB

In Philippians 2:1–12 Paul the apostle used the life of submission exemplified by Jesus as an example for believers everywhere to follow when he admonished the church to "let this mind be in you which was also in Christ Jesus" (v. 5, NKJV). Consequently if we are going to be like Jesus and empower others, we need to also submit to those in spiritual authority over us. If we cannot submit to spiritual authority, how can we expect the ones we are mentoring to submit to our leadership? We need to have more biblical understanding of this subject before we can understand the need for it in our own lives. This is especially important in this day and age when so many younger believers reject all vestiges of institutional authority, both spiritual and political, because of past abuses as well as because of the rebellious nature of our current cultural climate.

The Need for Spiritual Authority

Spiritual authority was established right from the beginning of human history, when God told Adam and Eve to steward the planet (Gen. 1:26–28). The fact that Adam represented the whole human race is clear from Romans

5:12, which says that when he sinned, all sinned; this is why we are by nature objects of God's wrath, as we see in Ephesians 2:1–3. This is called federal headship and can be understood in contemporary society when all the people of a nation are affected for good or evil by the decisions of their leader. For example, a nation can go to war against another nation because of its leaders. Hence, young men who have nothing to do with these decisions may die on the battlefield because their leaders decided to go to war.

Jesus spoke about delegated authority when He said, "Whoever receives you receives me" (Matt. 10:40). Thus, Jesus imparted not only His power but also His delegated authority in His leaders so His kingdom could be properly aligned. This is why He gave His leaders the power to bind and loose things on earth (Matt. 16:19). In plain English, when a person cannot submit to spiritual authority, he or she cannot submit to Jesus' leadership. Truly the church is the visible community of the invisible triune God. The Bible makes it very clear that there are leaders in the church. Paul says that apostles and prophets are the foundation of the church (Eph. 2:20). Ephesians 4:13 implies that we still need apostles and prophets and the whole fivefold ministry gifts today in order to mature.

Ephesians 4:7–12 teaches that the grace of God to be equipped for your purpose in Christ doesn't come directly from heaven to you but through the fivefold ministry. If you are not sitting under the fivefold gifts, you will not mature, even if you are saved. This illustrates how important your spiritual leaders and the church you attend are.

The measure of grace you receive is based upon the measure of grace the leader has that imparts to you.

Other leaders in the church are elders and deacons. Elders help shepherd, bear the burden of the church, and make decisions with the lead pastor. Together they form an eldership team (Num. 11:16–17). Deacons are recognized servants, as we see in Acts 6:1–7, whose focus is more on meeting the material needs of the church family. The Bible makes it clear that we need to be accountable to spiritual leaders in order to grow. The fifth commandment teaches us to honor our fathers and mothers, which implies both the spiritual and biological parents God has given you (Deut. 5:16). Hebrews 13:17 also teaches us to submit to our spiritual leaders. The Bible clearly teaches about the importance of receiving commandments from leaders, not just from God (Prov. 10:8, 17; 29:1).

Even Paul the apostle submitted his ministry and what he was preaching to the main apostles in Jerusalem, as we see in Galatians 2:1–2. Furthermore, going to older, mature believers in order to resolve conflict is important, as we see in Matthew 18:15–18. Young people need the input of older, seasoned believers in order to deal with certain relational issues and challenges in life, which is why this directs us to tell it to the elders. We should not gossip about, slander, or uncover our leaders, as demonstrated in Genesis 9:20–27, when one of Noah's sons was cursed for uncovering his father's nakedness instead of covering and protecting him. God held that son accountable, even though Noah was in the wrong for getting drunk and laying naked in his room.

We are called not only to have an individual walk with God but to walk in community with His household, which is led by spiritual leaders He assigns. If we cannot submit to them, then it shows we have a problem submitting to God. In a practical sense I have discovered that every person needs at least three functional areas of covering or oversight in his or her life in order to be whole.

The Need for Personal Covering

One thing many believers, including leaders, have in common is their lack of functional personal covering for their personal lives and ministries. By "personal covering" I am referring to having either an individual spiritual mentor or guide who serves as overseer who also has the authority to remove you or advocate for you in a time of moral failure or crisis. I don't usually use the term *covering* but rather *oversight* or *overseer* because those are the more biblical terms. But for the sake of common language with my audience, I am using the term *covering* in this chapter.

Many leaders, including myself, have one primary person who serves as their covering, who is also part of a group of leaders who serve as their presbytery. This type of primary person is one who holds the leader accountable and can serve as a mediator in case their standing as senior leader is in question, or if there is a need for mediation between them and their board of directors and leadership team.

This type of personal covering has to be relational. This means it will only work if the person is in regular dialogue with his overseer and is honest regarding his personal challenges. One major minister who fell into scandal a couple of years ago actually had a lot of close relationships and even prayed every morning with a close friend of mine. The problem was he never fully opened up regarding his dark side and sexual proclivities. Hence, having a close personal relationship with your overseer is never enough if you are not open and transparent with him. This is why I am using the modifier *functional* with "personal covering."

When a person doesn't have an honest, open, transparent relationship with a person who serves as the primary covering, it can be a disaster waiting to happen. All believers, including leaders, go through challenging times and need a person who can correct, encourage, rebuke, or exhort them to continue to pursue God's calling in their lives. Even if a lead pastor never falls into sin, he or she may be accused of a sinful act, and the church or organization may need to have an outside overseer or presbytery it can rely upon to investigate and/or mediate between both parties, to help sort out what is true from what is false and what strategic steps it should take for the good of the organization. Woe to the person who has no one to confide in, turn to for advice, remove him or her, or advocate in a time of crisis! In this context you can almost view covering as fire insurance: you never know if you will ever need it, but when a serious situation arises that can threaten your place in the church or organization, you will be thankful you had the foreknowledge to purchase it!

The lead pastors' pressing need for covering is one of the primary reasons I started Christ Covenant Coalition in 1999.[1] We are able to provide personal presbyteries for senior pastors in crisis as well as invaluable vertical and horizontal mentoring and covering.

The Need for Organizational Covering

Related to this, I believe every person needs to have organizational covering, which is usually provided by the elders or trustees of an organization. Along these lines, whenever any major decision is made related to vision and/or finances, every senior leader should first process it with these highly trusted leaders. I know many leaders who failed to do this and made major strategic or financial mistakes that in some cases cost them their ministries, all because they didn't enable their board of directors to be an intricate part of major decisions they were making. Several senior pastors I know went out on a limb in purchasing properties because "the Lord told them," making these decisions on their own, without consulting their elders or trustees. Unfortunately in most cases like this the leaders made huge blunders and even risked losing their whole ministries by plunging their work into huge debt because they didn't receive counsel from their trusted team of leaders. Even though I believe in one senior leader serving as the first among equals who can have the final say in important matters, I also believe in leading from consensus with your primary team as much as possible to protect the organization and the leader from making foolish mistakes that occur when functioning in isolation, not in cooperation with, your primary leaders. Also, when it comes to purchasing a building in which the whole congregation will be called upon to finance the vision, I believe it would also be wise for a senior pastor to hold a congregational meeting and receive the blessing of the whole church before proceeding forward with a large-scale building program.

The Need for a Prayer Covering

Another kind of covering that is essential for every person is a prayer covering. I have a regular team of people in our local church that is committed to praying daily for my wife, my family, and me. This has been essential the past two decades regarding our ability to persevere in the midst of life's challenges. Scripturally we also find that one of the primary parts of the armor of God is having the saints persevering in prayer for one another, even as Paul solicited prayers from the saints for his ministry (Eph. 6:18–20).

Recently the Lord spoke to me about the need to ramp up my prayer support because of a new sphere of influence and ministry I am walking into. With every new level there comes with it a higher devil. Thus, we need to pray and have intercession commensurate with the call of God upon our lives. Even though I usually spend a lot of private time seeking God every morning, I know I need outside help, which includes help from those functioning at a very high level in intercession on a national scale, to protect my family and me and enable me to press into every area of opportunity God opens up for me and my team.

For example, I remember reading nineteenth-century evangelist Charles Finney's autobiography and being impressed that he had personal intercessors (Father

Nash and Abel Clary) who would go ahead of him into every town and lock themselves in a room for days at a time, interceding and groaning in the Spirit with words that cannot be uttered in articulate speech, birthing in travail for revival. This was done even though Finney himself would usually spend hours every day seeking God and interceding for his ministry. This little-known fact is one of the primary reasons that Finney became the greatest revivalist the United States and perhaps the world has ever seen!

I posit that in order for every believer to be effective, we need to have at least three levels of covering: personal oversight, organizational oversight, and prayer covering that goes beyond our own prayer lives. If leaders function with this level of accountability, then their chances of failing or falling will be greatly diminished.

Three Relational Levels of Authority Needed

Along these lines of submission and oversight, I also believe every person needs to have three levels of spiritual authority operating in his or her life, just like a biological family. After all, the body of Christ is a family of families under Christ.

Everyone needs a spiritual parent.

Just as with a biological family, everyone needs to have a person functioning as a spiritual parent in his or her life to be healthy. If there isn't anybody who can hold you accountable, speak honestly to you, and even remove you from a ministry, then you are already treading in dangerous waters.

Everyone needs brothers and sisters they can trust.

Similar to a biological family, it is healthy for all people to have peers or brothers and sisters as friends and confidantes that person can trust and bounce things off of. Just having spiritual parents without brothers and sisters can be very lonely and not healthy. Just having brothers and sisters without a spiritual overseer is also not healthy.

Everyone needs sons and daughters to pour into.

Lastly, everyone should have at least one person he or she is mentoring and pouring into, whether the person is considered a spiritual child or not.

When we have all three of these levels operating at the same time, we have balance and are healthy spiritually, emotionally, and even materially.

In closing out this chapter, if you have a mentor without a personal overseer, you have the right to question him about why he has this lack. If it is because he does not want to personally submit to anyone, in my opinion this is not the kind of person you should have to mentor you. Also, if you attempt to mentor a person who does not desire any true accountability and oversight, you are wasting your time because potential cannot be unleashed and be successful long term without it being harnessed by accountability structures set in place.

Chapter 16

The Power of Prayer

IN EXAMINING THE Gospels, I find it fascinating that nowhere do we find a record of any of the disciples of Jesus asking Him how to preach, heal, or cast out demons. However, we do find them asking Him to teach them how to pray (Luke 11:1). I believe the reason for this is simple: they realized that the secret of His power was all the hours He spent alone praying and being in fellowship with His Father. He usually met God before He met men by getting up to pray before the morning light broke forth (Mark 1:35–36). Hence, He was continuously filled with the Spirit and the mind of His Father so that He could do the works of His Father.

Isaiah prophesied about the Messiah:

> The Lord GOD has given me the tongue of those who are taught, that I may know how to sustain with a word him who is weary. Morning by morning he

awakens; he awakens my ear to hear as those who
are taught. The Lord GOD has opened my ear, and I
was not rebellious; I turned not backward.

—ISAIAH 50:4–5

Jesus was able to unleash the potential in others because
He was always filled with the Holy Spirit and always
walking in the highest level of His own potential and power.
Consequently if we are going to help release potential in
others, we need to be continuously filled with the Holy Spirit
(Eph. 5:18) and have a robust prayer life of seeking God continually. If we are not on the top of our game, how can we
expect to release others to walk in their divine purpose?

Not only did Jesus pray to understand the power and
will of the Father, but He also lived a life of prayer for His
disciples. To this day, as our High Priest, He is continually
praying for all believers. As the writer to the Hebrews says,
"He always lives to make intercession for [us]" (7:25). Not
only that, but it was through praying all night that Jesus
knew whom to choose as His disciples (Mark 3:13–15). It
was living a life of prayer for His disciples that enabled
Jesus to have the wisdom to minister to them and sustain
them. In a previous chapter we already alluded to the fact
that Jesus was able to prophetically pray for Peter because
He knew in the spirit that Satan was about to tempt him
to fall away from being a Christ follower (Luke 22:31). He
realized that by continually praying for His disciples, He
was able to discern not only the will of God but the plans
of the evil one so He could thwart him.

Also, by keeping His disciples close by Himself when He prayed, Jesus was able to teach His disciples how to pray through and survive during the most difficult times in their lives. The fact that He made an impression on His disciples by the example of His prayer life is clearly seen as one of the profound descriptions of His life was given by the writer to the Hebrews when he said about Jesus, "In the days of His flesh, He offered up both prayers and supplications with loud crying and tears to the One able to save Him from death, and He was heard because of His piety" (Heb. 5:7, NASB). This probably points back to His intense prayer in the Garden of Gethsemane when Luke says about Him: "And being in agony He was praying very fervently; and His sweat became like drops of blood, falling down upon the ground" (Luke 22:44, NASB). There He taught His disciples to watch and pray lest they fall into temptation, because the spirit is willing, but the flesh is weak (Matt. 26:41).

I have found that the greatest way to teach a person to pray is for the person to pray with you or to attend powerful prayer gatherings. Truly prayer is caught more than taught! We can see that the example of Jesus' prayer life imprinted the life of the apostles by the way they led the early church. In the same way Jesus spent time praying during severe tests in His life, even so the apostles prayed until the house they were meeting in was shaken after they were threatened (Acts 4:24–31).

Furthermore, even before the church was born, the disciples spent ten full days continually praying, waiting upon God and examining the scriptures in the Upper Room, which resulted in the Holy Spirit falling upon the new church on the day of Pentecost (Acts 1–2). The numerous instances strewn throughout the Acts narrative connecting corporate and individual prayer to the miraculous spread of the gospel is so profound that we can almost call it "the book of prayer" instead of the Book of Acts! For example, one of the first descriptions of the early church was that "they devoted themselves to the apostles' teaching and the fellowship, to the breaking of bread and the prayer" (Acts 2:42).

It was when Peter and John were going to the temple during the hour of prayer that they met the lame man at the gate who was subsequently healed and was a catalyst for many thousands hearing the word and getting saved (Acts 3–4). It was the apostle Peter's insistence that the apostles devote themselves to prayer and the ministry of the Word, resulting in the further delegation of ministry and the birth of the office of deacon, which resulted in the Word of the Lord multiplying and the number of disciples being increased (Acts 6:1–7). It was Cornelius' prayer coupled with Peter's habit of prayer that enabled both of them to receive a word of the Lord that opened up the gospel to non-Jewish believers (Acts 10–11). It was when the leaders of the church in Antioch ministered to the Lord and fasted that the Spirit spoke to them to send Barnabas and Saul out to do apostolic missions, which became the start of the great church-planting movement that spread Christianity into Europe and changed the world (Acts 13:1–2).

When Paul and Silas went to a place of prayer, they met a woman named Lydia and won her to the Lord, which opened the door for the church to start in Western Europe. It was also when Paul and Silas were arrested; they worshipped and prayed, and the Lord sent an earthquake that opened the prison doors, resulting in the jailer and his whole family coming to Christ. (See Acts 16.)

This is just a snapshot of how the early church integrated the power of prayer into their daily lives, both as individuals and corporately as a church. After reading these accounts, coupled with the devotion of Jesus to prayer, to think that we can unleash potential in others without incorporating prayer is ludicrous. Just giving people Bible studies and getting them to go to church on Sunday is not enough. We have to pray for them! By praying for those we are mentoring, we are connected to their destiny and can help them discern the will of God and their calling. By praying for them, we are able to discern potential problems in their lives as well as imminent spiritual attacks. Paul admonishes the church, "With all prayer and petition pray at all times in the Spirit, and with this in view, be on the alert with all perseverance and petition for all the saints" (Eph. 6:18, NASB).

Praying for others connects you to their spirit instead of just seeing their actions. Thus, without prayer we will not be able to discern the true motives and spiritual condition of those we are mentoring. Whenever I am concerned about an individual I am mentoring, or whenever I am about to have a serious talk with him, I first seek the Lord to get His mind about the situation and the person, and He always gives me the proper perspective. Often God also gives me prophetic insight to share with that person that uncovers misconceptions, demonic lies, and deception, as well as presumptuous plans he is making that can derail him and his destiny. I often write down the things the Lord shows me before I meet with somebody I am mentoring, especially if I am concerned. Most of the time what I wrote down was exactly what that person was thinking regarding a situation or important decision in his life. When I showed him what the Lord gave me, he was often shocked and backed away from making a serious mistake. As mentioned in a previous chapter, sometimes people reject the Word of the Lord and do what they want anyway, resulting in huge mistakes in their lives.

Of course we are called to pray for our family and loved ones, not just those we are mentoring. In my book *Travail to Prevail* I recount numerous stories of how I was praying for one of my children, and God gave me prophetic warnings about serious situations that were about to occur that I was able to thwart in the spirit before they manifested. I knew it was a true warning from God because situations unfolded just as I said they would but with good instead of bad results! Consequently with the focus my wife, Joyce, and I have in prayer, my children have also cultivated strong prayer lives as a result. We always prayed with the family regularly as part of our family routine, but in addition to that our children see and hear how Joyce and I pray through to victory for every crisis.

They have also witnessed miraculous healings and answers to prayers throughout the years that have sustained our family! Recently one of my sons and his wife were told that one of their unborn twins was not getting enough blood because the placenta was not functioning. They wanted to deliver the twins at twenty-seven weeks, which could be potentially dangerous for their survival and health. My wife, my oldest son, and I then commenced to get dozens of people on prayer calls for the next six weeks, and every time the doctors checked on the babies, there was an ample supply of blood coming to them. By the grace and glory of God the twins were not removed from the womb until they were almost at thirty-three weeks. When they took the babies out, they found that there was not one drop of blood in the placentas! God miraculously sustained these babies in the womb until the proper time for them to come forth!

Our children have been exposed to this and numerous other stories like this in both the church and our family since they were born, resulting in them understanding the importance of having a life of prayer and faith. The result is that when they have their own families (like my two sons already do), they will also pass this lifestyle of prayer and faith to their children's children, and the cycle of prayer and faith will continue for generations.

I remember one salient example of the imprint prayer has had on my children. One time one of my daughters came to me confused and asked me why another family in the church (she was friends with their daughter) did not fast and pray for their children the way we do. Since she was raised to live this way, she thought it was normal for Christian families to regularly pray together and believe

God for their children. When she did not see this being lived out in another believing family, she was shocked! If we are going to unleash potential the way Jesus did, we need to pray and seek the Father the way He did, which is also how the early church functioned in the Book of Acts. If we follow everything else written in this book but fail at this one point, we will also fail at every other point!

Chapter 17

Ending Well

THIS BOOK WOULD not be complete unless I included a chapter on ending well. Truly it is not how you start but how you finish in life that matters. One of the most important things Jesus taught His disciples was to finish well— to have a goal that they would end their lives walking in divine purpose. He never attempted to nurture men who would become "shooting stars," people who start off with a big bang but crash and burn as fast as they went up!

Consequently this book would not be complete if we did not include some principles for finishing well in our life journey. There have been great leadership books on living a significant life and finishing well. (*Halftime: Moving From Success to Significance* by Bob Buford is one that comes to mind.) In this chapter I want to focus especially on how we who mentor others can finish well. After all, if we do not practice principles of finishing well, how are we going to help others fulfill their potential and walk in their divine purpose and calling?

One of the saddest conversations I ever had was with several older leaders who confided in me that most leaders they knew never finished well. This caused me to start looking around and having as many conversations as I could with older leaders regarding this subject. By "finishing well" I am referring to fulfilling the work that God gave us (John 17:4) so that we pass into the next world satisfied (Ps. 91:16).

Paul said regarding his final days:

> For I am already being poured out as a drink offering, and the time of my departure has come. I have fought the good fight, I have finished the race, I have kept the faith. Henceforth there is laid up for me the crown of righteousness, which the Lord, the righteous judge, will award to me on that day, and not only to me but also to all who have loved his appearing.
>
> —2 TIMOTHY 4:6–8

The following are some principles that enable us to finish well.

Leave a legacy of faith, courage, and integrity.

In order to finish well, we need to live lives of faith and courage with no major regrets that we missed the purpose of God in our lives because we were afraid to take risks and believe God. Furthermore, we need to cultivate lives of integrity without engaging in scandalous behavior, which will come back to bite us later in life, clouding our legacies.[1]

Adequately equip the next generation of leaders God sends you.

There is perhaps nothing more important for finishing well than to take aside people with potential and pour into them so that you are always reproducing yourself in those with capacity to influence many others. The main agenda of Jesus was to pour into the twelve apostles, not the large crowds that gathered to hear Him preach.

Pastors who focus on preaching to and gathering crowds instead of choosing a remnant of people to equip will not finish well, because at the end of the day you want your disciples to be doing greater works than you before you pass on to the next life. People will die unsatisfied if they don't see their spiritual children excelling in life and ministry.

Successfully transition through the four leadership stages in life.

There are at least four leadership stages in life. Most people never get past the second stage.

The first stage is to be a leader other people can follow. This involves using your gifts to draw a crowd, preach the gospel, and create a community of people who follow Jesus.

The second stage is to develop leaders who can produce other leaders. Unfortunately most leaders barely scratch the surface regarding this stage because they want to be the ones doing all the preaching, praying, weddings, funerals, and hospital visitations; they need to feel needed. Yet those who don't enter this second stage have violated 2 Timothy 2:2, which teaches that we need to focus on developing those few people who are able to teach others.

The third stage is to allow those leaders you have developed to lead so they can develop their own leaders while you focus on coaching the leaders of leaders. This usually happens once a leader is in his or her forties or fifties, after becoming a seasoned leader with more than two decades' leadership experience. Each stage can take almost a decade to move into!

The fourth and final stage, during the final two to three decades of life, is to concentrate on being a mentor to leaders who oversee networks and movements and leaders who oversee leaders of leaders. Very few reach this last stage. It may also be true that only a few leaders are even called to reach this fourth stage of leadership. Those called to transition into this stage will not be satisfied in their final days on the earth if they have not walked in this level. What may be considered successful to some leaders may not be for others called to higher levels of leadership.

Surround yourself with spiritual sons and daughters who carry your DNA.

At the end of the day the crowds come and go, but those you have nurtured as spiritual sons and daughters will always be devoted to you. Perhaps the greatest regret of some believers is that they did not adequately parent the children God gave them, resulting in their having no spiritual children in their later years.

Some older Christians have even said their greatest regret was not spending more time pouring into younger people, because when they hit their eighties, most, if not all, of their peers were dead, and they were left alone with no true friends. In order to finish well, we need to develop and mentor young people who will carry our DNA into the next generation.

Adequately journal the main life lessons you have learned, to pass them on to others.

Perhaps one of the things believers can do to maximize the impact they will have for the future is to journal their life experiences so that future leaders can glean from them. For example, the autobiography of Charles Finney, the journals of John Wesley and David Brainerd, and the writings of Jonathan Edwards and others have greatly aided in my personal development. I don't know where I would be today if I didn't have the writings that document their lives. Perhaps they have had more influence through what they documented for future generations than when they were alive.

I believe in order to finish well, we need to at least document the major lessons we have learned. Many may also be called to write at least one book that teaches their life message. Taking five to ten minutes a day to journal lessons learned or things God spoke to your soul can be a powerful force for good for your biological and spiritual children, who will be clamoring for your writings after you pass on to the next world.

Love your spouse and biological children.

One of the greatest regrets of older leaders is having lost their families to the world because they neglected them due to the enormity of the work they had to do. It will be easier to finish well knowing that we loved our spouses and children to the end, lived sacrificially for them, and did our best to lead them into the way of the kingdom of God.

What good is it if we win the whole world but lose our children to the world? I don't want my children cursing me at my graveside or refusing to come to my funeral because I left them with a bitter taste for God, the church, and myself, and because I lived hypocritically by feigning love for God and people in public while neglecting them in private.

Carry no grudges.

In order to finish well, we need to have a clean slate in our hearts toward those we have worked with. We need to have short accounts with others and walk in the principles of Matthew 18:15–17 so that if we have something against our brother or sister, we will immediately speak to him or her and attempt to resolve it instead of talking about that person and having unforgiveness in our hearts. Believers who don't walk in the light with others will carry unresolved issues that can result in bitterness. We can't walk around in bitterness and resentment, blaming other people for our lack of success or fulfillment in life.

We also need to make sure we don't allow other people

to control our emotions by their actions. Despite what others may say and do to us, we need to forgive them and have clean and pure hearts before God so we can pass into glory in peace. Bitter people usually don't finish well; they finish angry and unsatisfied!

Point everyone to Jesus and not to yourself.

Finally, finishing well ultimately depends upon whether we lived lives to glorify and bring attention to ourselves or to Jesus. The greatest thing someone can say about us at our funeral will be that we loved God and caused others to love God. More important than us being known for our preaching, large organizations, books, or accomplishments is that we inspired our biological families, our churches, and our generation to love and know God passionately!

There are many more things that can be written about finishing well. These are just a handful of ideas I have presented based on my limited experience and narrow perspective. May God help us all finish well!

Chapter 18

Transformational Questions
to Ask Yourself
(For both mentor and mentee)

As we begin to close out this book, it is best that you ask yourself a set of questions that can help unearth issues that have to be dealt with. Without transformational questions to work with—something that radically alters your life— you will lack self-awareness and have no practical steps to apply the principles of Jesus you learned in this book.

Of course the following questions are important for both mentor and mentee if we are going to be self-aware and capable of unleashing potential in others.

Am I involved in an activity without purpose?

Often we make the mistake of thinking that much activity is equal to productivity. Sometimes the busiest people can be the most unproductive people because they major on the trivial things in life instead of the most important things. We all have to discern between *good things* and *God things* to do.

Do I value programs more than the people around me? (a question for a lead pastor)

Often leaders are so institutionally minded that they focus most of their energy on developing programs rather than investing in developing the people around them. Biblically speaking, Jesus did not build a huge organization. He built a great leadership team that would eventually create the greatest movement the world has ever seen.

Am I seeking God commensurate with the call and assignment of God in my life?

The more influential you become, the more opportunities will come your way that can crowd God out of your world. We should never be too busy to pray! God can only trust us with true influence based on our understanding of His ways and intimate knowledge of His person.

Am I solely focused on the outer world of goals, objectives, and accomplishments, or am I also paying attention to my inner man regarding my call to grow in love, humility, and living for the glory of God?

Since most people desire to always be in control, it is easy for them to live a life obsessed with objectives and accomplishments as a gauge to value their worth. The Bible teaches us clearly in 1 Corinthians 13 that the greatest pursuit to have is the pursuit of love, which assumes spiritual and emotional maturity. This comes only through paying more attention to our motives and emotional health, out of which arises spiritual vibrancy, than to mere accomplishments and objectives.

Am I investing enough of my time into the key relationships God has given me?

Jesus said in John 17:12 that of all the people the Father gave Him, He lost none. Jesus always focused most of His attention toward the twelve apostles the Father gave Him to disciple.

To maximize our purpose, we need to invest the proper amount of time in our spouses, biological children, spiritual children, and key people God has called us to build His kingdom with.

Do I recognize the season of life I am currently in?

Everybody is in a different season of life approximately every twenty years. Often leaders in their seventies and eighties are still trying to accomplish things those in their twenties and thirties should be doing. Those in their twenties and fifties are focusing on success, but those in their later years should be focused on significance, which primarily comes from mentoring younger people.

Am I continually cultivating the habit patterns necessary to achieve the maximum amount of efficiency?

Our destiny is determined by the habit patterns we have cultivated throughout our lives. We have to continually ask ourselves if we are focusing on developing the habits connected to our ultimate purpose in life. Often people spend more time with hobbies they are passionate about than developing habits necessary to fulfill their destiny.

For example, you may love to play golf, but if you are spending hours every day cultivating your game instead of doing what you are called to do, then you are putting something that is merely a hobby before your purpose in life.

Do I care for the health of my spirit, soul, and body?

Often believers neglect one major area of their lives because they are focused solely on another area. I have seen many Christians neglect their health with poor eating habits, a lack of sleep, or a lack of exercise. Their ensuing health problems limit their capacity to unleash potential or result in their premature death. God wants us to give equal attention to the development of good habits related to our spiritual life, emotional health, and physical health. Neglecting just one of these areas will greatly limit your ability to fulfill God's purpose in your life (1 Thess. 5:23).

Am I a good steward of my time, money, and the gifts and talents given to me?

God has given each of us a certain measure of gifts, talents, and abilities. We will all be judged as stewards of these gifts God entrusted to us. To whom much is given much more will be required on the day of judgment. Too many Christians allow major gifts and talents they have to remain dormant! Whatever God is giving you, you are responsible to develop and maximize for His glory.

Am I surrounding myself with the people who can bring me to the next level of His purpose?

I can usually predict a person's trajectory by checking out the people closest to them. Those who hang out with bitter people will become bitter. Those who hang out with lazy people will become lazy. Those who hang out with high achievers will themselves have a better chance of maximizing their abilities. Most importantly, surround yourself with the proper mentors and friends who will inspire you to go to the next level in life. Your closest confidants should be those who call upon the Lord out of a pure heart and seek first His kingdom and His righteousness.

In closing, every mentor needs a mentor to help him or her unleash his or her full potential. My prayer for all who read this book is that you will find an uncommon mentor who will help release the fullness of your purpose in life, which is to become like Jesus. My prayer is also that as you freely receive from the Lord, you will also freely give to others so that they also can walk in the fullness of their purpose.

Appendix

Effective Ways to Help
Mature Christ Followers

IN ORDER TO mentor people the way Jesus did, we need to understand the fact that Jesus never enabled or empowered people comfortable in their sin or bad attitudes. That is to say, He was tough with His disciples when He needed to be tough and corrected them when they needed correction. Mentors must be willing to give constructive criticism to those they are pouring into, or they will forfeit the role God has given them to help shape those particular people. Mentors who are afraid of godly confrontation or refuse to bring correction to those they are mentoring will be guilty of helping perpetuate habit patterns harmful to those people God has entrusted to them. These are mentors who desire to please people more than help people.

This is a tendency the apostle Paul spoke against (1 Thess. 2:4).

After more than forty years of teaching and mentoring others, I have come to the conclusion that there are two kinds of disciple makers or mentors in the body of Christ: enablers and those who disciple. In the following section I am going to contrast enablers and true disciple makers so that you will be able to discern which category you fit in. If you are in the enabler category, my prayer is that after reading this section, you will turn away from this style of leadership and transition toward true, biblical disciple making. Since much of discipleship takes place in the context of small groups in a local church, I have crafted these contrasts to fit the small-group dynamic. However, they can be applied in a one-on-one setting as well as other settings.

Traits of an Enabler

Enablers accommodate their message and approach to ministry based on the commitment level of their group rather than keeping biblical standards. Hence, their goal is to keep people happy and not make anyone uncomfortable. The challenge with this approach is the fact that it is the mentors, not the mentees, who should determine the standards and content of the teachings (content that always conforms to Scripture).

Can you imagine what would have happened had the Lord Jesus based the standard of His teachings on the value system of those He was teaching? This point is even more important today since we are in the midst of cultural and moral decline and often those in the church have adopted values and views that counter rather than conform to the Word of God. Of course every mentor, like Jesus, should use language and examples familiar to those they are teaching to make it easier for them to assimilate and understand. When Jesus was with those familiar with an agrarian culture, He spoke about sowing seeds, lost sheep, and being the Good Shepherd. When He was with the woman at the well, He spoke to her about living water and so forth. Consequently a good mentor should utilize the language of culture to make a point without compromising biblical standards and values. Even when Jesus was eating and drinking with sinners, He never compromised His message and essence by coming down to their level of behavior. He was a bridge builder between sinners and the Father so that He would draw people unto God. He was always the "table setter," not vice versa.

Enablers rarely challenge those they mentor even when they have been saved a long time and are not adhering to the foundational principles of attending church, sharing their faith, tithing, giving offerings, living holy lives, and seeking first the kingdom of God. I have known small-group leaders and so-called mentors who never make a difference regarding the behavior and goals of mentees. Of course at the end of the day I believe every person has to choose the kind of life he or she is trying to lead. However, irrespective of who is mentoring them, I have seen some people who are effective in shaping and motivating the lives of people they are mentoring and others who only provide good fellowship without challenging the status quo. Good mentors, more often than not, will have a positive impact on the lives and trajectory of those they are mentoring.

Enablers rarely integrate the ministry and vision of their local congregation but instead empower unaccountable individualism. Enablers tend to point to themselves rather than to the vision of the local church. This is due to the fact that what is motivating them the most is obtaining the love and affection of people. Consequently both mentor and mentee and/or small group develop a fleshly emotional bond that becomes codependent. The result is that the small group or mentees become more committed to their mentor than to the church vision and to Jesus. They become islands unto themselves, even in the context of serving in a church ministry. Codependent mentor-mentee dynamics result in the mentor drawing disciples after themselves instead of integrating their ministry with the vision of the local church. Of course when there is more than one vision in a local church, there is division, and trouble is not far behind.

Another trait of enablers is they continually make excuses for those they are ministering to when they are operating outside of God's will—for example, they are too busy to attend church on Sundays, tithing isn't important because God just wants their hearts first, and so on. Truth be told, there will always be a way to justify disobedience to God. When was it ever easy for Jesus and the original apostles, or for any one of us, for that matter? No, those we mentor sometimes fall into deception and disobedience to Christ, and they always attempt to hide behind good excuses and difficult circumstances.

One of the primary jobs of a Christlike mentor is to uncover the root reasons behind these "good excuses" and challenge mentees to serve God even in the midst of trials and hardships. This is why the apostle Paul said to Timothy, "Share in suffering as a good soldier of Christ Jesus" (2 Tim. 2:3). A Christlike mentor is going to teach mentees that God allows hardships to test the faith of believers and to see if they really want to serve Him despite their many obstacles and challenges (Jas. 1:2–4).

Enablers will not only empathize with the poor excuses of their mentees but also sympathize with them and affirm many decisions deleterious to their faith and calling. Thus, because these enablers, perhaps unintentionally, are reinforcing the disobedient lifestyle of their mentees, either because of their own lack of conviction and/or passion in these dark areas or because the desire and need for them to be liked outweighs their motivation to disagree, they do not confront and help conform mentees to the image of Christ. Of course confrontation should always be done in love, grace, and mercy, and yet it has to be done, or mentees will feel empowered in their disobedience rather than convicted.

Finally enablers sympathize rather than empathize with mentees when they complain about spiritual authority and leadership. This perhaps is the most destructive trait of an enabler. This is because they have betrayed the trust given them by the spiritual leaders of a local church by entertaining accusations or complaints about spiritual authority in their congregation. Everybody knows that it is very easy to criticize leadership, whether political or church leadership, when you are not the person responsible for steering the ship. We can all second-guess leaders, criticize their teachings, leadership style, or interaction with people they are in conflict with. Mentors who enable this kind of behavior function like Absalom, the son of David who stole the hearts of the people of Israel before they turned on their king (2 Sam. 15).

It is the role of mentors to understand how to correctly represent the spiritual authority of a local church and to point mentees to Matthew 18:15–17 if and when they believe a spiritual leader has wronged them. Failure to promote biblical transparency (1 John 1:5–7) with mentees is to willingly participate in divisive actions that can harm both the mentee and the church.

The Biblical Traits of a Christlike Mentor

Christlike mentors should point people to Jesus, not to themselves. The primary objective of all biblical mentors is getting people to a right place in God's purposes rather than having them love their mentor and agree with that person on everything. Sometimes this means that the mentor has to have difficult conversations with the mentee regarding his or her lack of commitment to God and to biblical standards.

While enablers will avoid confrontational conversations at all costs, Christlike mentors push through the awkwardness to have difficult discussions for the sake of the soul of the mentee. Consequently Christlike mentors never intentionally hold back presenting the whole counsel of God. They consistently teach on things culturally uncomfortable, such as living a sexually pure lifestyle, keeping the Lord's day first instead of family events (related to participation with the congregation of the Lord every Sunday), and giving tithes and offerings to support the work of God's kingdom, to name a few typical issues.

Christlike mentors also continually pray for their church, their spiritual leadership, and for the vision of their local church in their group meetings so that all in proximity to them are inextricably connected to the life and vision of their church. Furthermore, they eventually (when they deem them ready) encourage mentees to volunteer to serve in the ministry of the church so that they are learning how to use their gifts and talents for the Lord.

They also challenge and coach mentees regarding having a private devotional life with the Lord and a devotional life with their family. They teach, model, and exhort mentees to walk in forgiveness and build lasting covenant relationships with their immediate family and church family (not based on a self-centered "I, me, my" existence) by training them to keep putting others before themselves, just as Jesus did, as it says in Philippians 2:1–8. Ultimately Christlike mentors empower others to reproduce themselves by winning people to Christ and making disciples instead of just barely hanging on with the Lord in survival mode with a goal of just having peace in their lives, having their needs met, and making it to heaven, as many Christians do.

The goal of a Christlike mentor is to eventually feed mentees meat, not milk, as is commanded by Paul in 1 Corinthians 3:1–3 and Hebrews 5:12. In spite of passages such as Hebrews 6:1–4, some of us are still teaching those who have been saved for years as if they are new Christians! Finally when it comes to building covenant and making disciples, we are stewards of Christ and of His gospel—the most privileged and most awful responsibility in the world! The call of the church is not to have a nonconfrontational social club like the local pub but to have a countercultural social army of disciples! We are called to be on the front lines of prayer, fasting, evangelism, discipleship, and societal transformation. Sadly much of the body of Christ has been on the front lines of accommodating the needs and desires this consumption-obsessed culture imposes on the population. Our call is not to make everybody happy but to exhort all to be purposeful! Although we are called to minister to the emotional needs of people, we have to do it on God's terms of discipleship and commitment, not on humanistic, self-centered terms that have no ultimate goal except self-preservation and pleasure.

It is important for those we mentor to love us. However, they will not always like us in the process. Thus, it is more important to please God than men, as Paul said in his epistles. God is with us, and His Spirit will empower us *if we are His witnesses* and not witnesses to ourselves and our own desires (Acts 1:8). If you want to please all people, become an entertainer, not a leader!

In retrospect, serving as a Christlike mentor is perhaps the greatest privilege any of us will ever have (besides worship) this side of heaven. We need to count the cost and understand the exceedingly great requirements of modeling leadership to others before we commence this task. We should study the Scriptures and see how leaders such as Moses, Samuel, and David in the Old Testament, and Jesus and Paul in the New Testament processed and matured believers so we can follow their examples. We need to study key passages related to leadership that can serve as a guide for our own lives and mentoring ministry.[1]

Finally, although Paul teaches that the five cluster gifts of apostle, prophet, pastor, teacher, and evangelist, which are ministry functions mentioned in Ephesians 4:11, are primarily ministries called to equip believers (v. 12), Scripture makes it clear that God expects all believers to reproduce themselves and make disciples irrespective of what assignment they have in the kingdom of God (Matt. 28:19–20). All believers are called to be equipped in the church place so they can make disciples in the workplace in addition to discipling their biological families. We are primarily called to impart to others as we do life with them (Deut. 6:6–9) because Christianity is not an institutional religion but based upon the way of Jesus and His teachings (John 14:6). Hence, if we limit disciple making to organized church meetings, we will miss out on utilizing the time and space we share with those we spend most of our time with at school or at work.

All believers—whether they are called to be in full-time church ministry or not—are called to be His ministers wherever they are so that they can equip Christ followers in every sector of society. If every believer in the next year would merely win one person and disciple him or her, then Christianity would explode and double in size in just one year!

As an addendum to this book related to helping shape and draw out the best in the lives of Christ followers, I have collapsed my teaching on making disciples down to ten laws, to make it easier to follow. This is based on my more than four decades of disciple making, mentoring, and helping release believers to their divine destiny and calling.

Ten Laws for Effective Disciple Making

1. Be relational.

One of the biggest needs in the body of Christ today is for spiritual leaders to socially relate to those they are mentoring. It is not enough just to mentor people in the typical environment of a church meeting or service. Often spiritual leaders are unapproachable outside of the context of the church service. I have found that those I take under my wing grow the fastest when I invest personal time with them and pour into them.

When spiritual leaders can only relate to those they are mentoring in the context of an organized church service, then it may be a sign of a social dysfunction in the mentor since it is not natural to only relate in religious settings. Unfortunately some leaders are insecure and only feel comfortable with their followers when they stand behind the pulpit "under the anointing" and are in a position of power without the vulnerability of open conversation, dialogue, and unpredictable social dynamics.

When we examine the Gospels, we see that spending time with Jesus was one of the major components related to His method of disciple making. In Mark 3:14 and John 1:38–39 we see how Jesus invited His followers to spend time with Him so they could see and experience what it was like to be with Him. His preaching and teaching were only part of the method He employed for disciple making. Actually His teaching and preaching only supplemented their constant proximity to Him. This is why John wrote in his first epistle regarding Jesus, "That which was from the beginning, which we have heard, which we have seen with our eyes, which we looked upon and touched with our hands, concerning the word of life" (1 John 1:1).

2. Do life together.

Along with the first point, we need to understand that disciple making is really about integrating and intertwining lives together so that we begin to do life together. That is to say, to truly make disciples, we need to make those we are mentoring part of our lives. Jesus did not merely teach people once per week in a religious service; He taught them while He was sitting with them on a mountain (Matt. 5:1) and while He was walking in the grain fields (Luke 6:1). He exemplified faith by how He responded to a life-threatening situation (Matt. 8:23–27). He taught how to handle ministry failure by how He responded when His leaders failed to effectively deliver a boy from demonic oppression (Mark 9:14–23), how He acted in the midst of leadership betrayal (Luke 22:20–34), and how He acted when His heart was extremely heavy with sorrow (Luke 22:39–46). By examining the life of Jesus, we see that perhaps His most effective way of maturing His followers was by simply allowing them to do life with Him.

3. Be committed to your mentee's success.

Even as Jesus washed His disciples' feet (John 13:1–20), so we are called to wash the feet of those we are called to disciple and mentor by being committed to their success. Unfortunately some leaders' idea of disciple making is limited to working with those who enable them to meet their personal and ministry objectives. Hence, they objectify people and use them instead of getting behind them and helping them reach their potential.

I have found that as I commit myself to helping people fulfill their calling, the blessing of God upon me is released in a way that activates all my gifts and abilities and brings me into the realm of God's favor, in which He in turn sends many people to help me walk out my calling and purpose. Not only that, when people know you truly care about them and want to help them fulfill their calling, they in turn will care about you and help you fulfill your vision.

Jesus said, "Freely you have received, freely give" (Matt. 10:8, NKJV), because there is so much of God's gifts and blessings to go around that we will never hurt our own calling by being committed to serving another person's calling! The more we faithfully give, the more we will receive from God because His well never runs dry! (See John 4:13–14; 7:38.)

4. Don't feel threatened by your mentee's success.

Perhaps the greatest testament to our success as mentors is when our mentees exceed our own ministry success. Jesus alluded to this when He said that His followers would do even greater works than He did (John 14:12). The greatest imprint of our lives will be the legacy of influence we have through our sons and daughters after we leave this world.

It is unfortunate that many leaders are like Absalom, whose only legacy was to erect a monument to himself because he had no sons (2 Sam. 18:18). Some pastors and leaders think that their greatest legacy will be the huge buildings they built; however, the greatest impact we will ever have is the deposit of the faith and vision we instill in our followers who will continue the mission of Jesus for generations to come. This is why Paul said to Timothy, "Follow the pattern of the sound words that you have heard from me, in the faith and love that are in Christ Jesus. By the Holy Spirit who dwells within us, guard the good deposit entrusted to you" (2 Tim. 1:13–14). He also told Timothy, "The things you have heard me say in the presence of many witnesses entrust to reliable people who will also be qualified to teach others" (2 Tim. 2:2, NIV).

Consequently the Pauline method of disciple making became an endless cycle of disciples making disciples who make disciples for generations to come! This is why the church has continued to thrive more than two millennia after its inception! The greatest investment of Paul's time was with those he poured into, not the building of huge edifices, which is why right before his martyrdom Paul's final remarks to Timothy included these words:

> You, however, have followed my teaching, my conduct, my aim in life, my faith, my patience, my love, my steadfastness, my persecutions and sufferings that happened to me at Antioch, at Iconium, and at Lystra—which persecutions I endured; yet from them all the Lord rescued me. Indeed, all who desire to live a godly life in Christ Jesus will be persecuted, while evil people and impostors will go on from bad to worse, deceiving and being deceived. But as for you, continue in what you have learned and have firmly believed, knowing from whom you learned it.
>
> —2 TIMOTHY 3:10–14

It is obvious Paul's life was a model to shape the lives of countless disciples, who turned the world upside down (Acts 17:6), planted thousands of churches, and caused the mission of Jesus to flourish even until the present day. I'm sure Paul had no idea the kind of influence he would have for thousands of years to come, which primarily came about because he prepared those he mentored to do greater works than he did, so "though he died, he still speaks" (Heb. 11:4). To end this point, John said that he had no greater joy than when he saw his children walking in the truth (3 John 4). This is the kind of attitude all true mentors should have since it is the same attitude exhibited by the Lord Jesus throughout His ministry.

5. Be a "door opener" for your mentee.

One of the things that has astonished me through the years is how many people I have taken under my wing who have seen their lives and ministries explode with impact and influence. I cannot name all the people I know whose ministries took off after they became aligned with me through mentoring, and several have even become household names. This is because, when a person becomes apostolically aligned, his or her gifts, abilities, and calling are harnessed for maximum impact.

Often I notice the raw potential in people, and by giving them some guidance, accountability, and structure, they are able to flourish. Also, an important component of what occurs during the process of alignment with me is that they are able to connect with the people who can help take them to the next level in their workplace or church-place vocation. Sometimes I intentionally serve them as a "door opener" by introducing them to people I know can aid them. Or sometimes it is because they attend a conference I am facilitating (because they are aligned with me) and God orchestrates divine connections for them because He knows He can now trust them with influence because they have proper accountability and mentoring.

That being said, one of the roles of a good mentor is to be a "door opener" by granting people "the gift of access," access that took me years building relational capital with significant people to acquire and that in an instant I can grant a mentee I trust by allowing him or her to use my name to connect with someone significant. I have great joy when I am able to connect those I mentor with others who can help them fulfill their God-given dreams. This is absolutely one of the roles every mentor should have.

6. Think outside the box when it comes to discipling.

Through the years, as my traveling schedule became more demanding, I realized I had less time to pour into others in a local setting. To help compensate for this, I started asking leaders I was mentoring to take ministry trips with me—some as long as a week or longer. I discovered that this is an incredibly effective way of making disciples because it combines various elements crucial to shaping lives.

For example, they get to hear my teaching for an extended amount of time in a conference setting (not merely for an hour Bible study or Sunday message). They get to hang out with me while traveling and sharing meals together; they get to debrief the meetings with me; they get to help me discern what the Lord was saying and doing in the midst of those I was ministering to; they get exposed to foreign cultures, which takes them out of their comfort zone; and they get to meet some of the top leaders and most interesting people in the world, which further sharpens their ax and accelerates their process of spiritual formation.

Consequently I have learned to think outside the box and adapt disciple making to the ever-changing realities of my life. If I failed to do this, then my disciple making would have greatly diminished when I started itinerating with extra local ministry. I have found that one week of traveling with me in ministry was equal to more than six months of weekly Bible studies and regular services. Rather than quit the disciple-making component of my life because of excessive travel, in some ways my mentoring has become more effective because I can often take one or more people with me on a ministry trip and see how quickly God can transform a person's life.

7. Process decisions together to develop critical thinking.

If all I do is dictate to those I mentor, I will merely produce followers. However, if I want to produce and multiply other leaders, I have to make them part of the decision-making process so they can learn critical thinking, which in turn will enable them to problem-solve, take initiative, and be innovative in their approach.

When I have new believers I am pouring into, I am limited in regard to how much of the decision-making process they can participate in until we develop mutual trust and they mature as Christ followers. However, the more they mature, the more I attempt to allow them into higher level decision-making processes so they can learn firsthand the multitude of things they have to take into consideration when making an informed decision. They also learn how to operate in the context of the counsel of a team rather than operating in the vacuum of isolation. This is vital to develop balanced, mature Christ followers who will in turn become effective leaders and mentors.

8. Process strategic planning together.

Along with decision-making, it is important to eventually include mentees in a strategic-planning process. This will take decision-making to another level and will better equip them in regard to going from A to Z in every aspect of their lives, businesses, and ministry. It is also important as part of the disciple-making process to teach mentees the difference between leadership and management; and how to distinguish between purpose, mission, goals, strategies, and tactics; and the role of each in the strategic-planning process.

I have found that some of the most anointed, gifted people I have ever met were capped in regard to their influence and productivity because they did not understand how to make their vision a reality. Truly, having a vision without the capacity to make it a reality is wasting creativity, innovation, and dreams. We have to teach mentees that great vision and anointing are usually never enough without a good administrative process that aptly turns a blueprint into the desired construct.

9. Give your mentee an opportunity to put your teachings into practice.

Jesus always began "to do and teach" (Acts 1:1). He never merely taught. Hence, true mentorship involves giving disciples the opportunity to apply your teachings by serving in the context of the Jesus community so there can be accountability and further instruction. (See this method of Jesus in Luke 9:1–2, 10; 10:1, 17–20).

In the context of overseeing a local church for several

decades, I have found that a Christ follower will stop growing a year or two after his or her conversion if the person does not volunteer to serve in the context of the congregation. Jesus said His food was to do the will of the Father (John 4:34). This goes against the grain of contemporary Christianity, which often teaches that our "meat" is merely hearing teaching after teaching instead of applying what we were taught. Even the apostle James said that faith without works is dead and that if we just hear the Word without being doers of the Word, we deceive ourselves (Jas. 2:17; 1:22).

In closing out this point, if we are going to make disciples the way Jesus did, we are going to look for the opportunity for our mentees to serve in some capacity that is observable, accountable, measurable, and goal oriented so that we can gauge their growth and maximize their potential for spiritual formation and service in the kingdom.

10. Encourage and walk in transparency in the relationship.

Last, but not least, we must establish transparency in our mentoring relationships to produce an environment of trust suitable for growth. I have found that the more mentees trust their mentors, the more they will grow because they will not hide their faults and will feel comfortable disclosing the deep dealings of God within their souls. Anything less than transparency is nothing more than a performance-based religious experience that will not amount to true Christian growth and maturity. As a matter of fact, according to Scripture, people cannot grow in Christ unless they walk in the light as He is in the light so that they can experience true fellowship with both God and His body (1 John 1:7).

I have found that there is nothing that develops greater trust, loyalty, and alignment with disciples than when I share my struggles and challenges and earnestly solicit their support and corporate prayer so we can together fulfill the will of God to advance His kingdom. Of course the more spiritually mature a mentee is, the more intimate details I can share, and the more mutual trust we can develop. This in turn results in amazing synergy that arises out of our oneness, which will continue to be held together by our continual commitment to walk in transparency. Without this vital component in our relationship, the mentoring dynamic will be greatly hindered and limited in its results.

In closing, my prayer is that these ten points will serve as guideposts capable of accelerating the disciple-making process for you and contribute to the rapid spread of the mission of Jesus in the earth today.

May the Lord of the harvest continue to produce Christlike mentors to equip the saints for the work of the ministry.

Notes

Chapter 1
Understanding Your God-Given Identity

1. Blue Letter Bible, s.v. *"Petros,"* accessed May 17, 2019, https://www.blueletterbible.org/lang/lexicon/lexicon. cfm?Strongs=G4074&t=KJV.
2. Blue Letter Bible, s.v. *"petra,"* accessed May 17, 2019, https://www.blueletterbible.org/lang/lexicon/lexicon. cfm?Strongs=G4073&t=KJV.
3. Blue Letter Bible, s.v. *"Abram,"* accessed May 17, 2019, https://www.blueletterbible.org/lang/lexicon/lexicon. cfm?Strongs=H87&t=KJV; Blue Letter Bible, s.v. *"Abraham,"* accessed May 17, 2019, https://www.blueletterbible.org/lang/ lexicon/lexicon.cfm?Strongs=H85&t=KJV.
4. Susan Reynolds, "Happy Brain, Happy Life," *Psychology Today*, August 2, 2011, https://www.psychologytoday.com/us/blog/ prime-your-gray-cells/201108/happy-brain-happy-life.
5. Reynolds, "Happy Brain, Happy Life."

Chapter 2
Unleashing Your Potential

1. Kristian David Hernandez's book, *Beholding and Proclaiming: Reimaging the Art of Preaching and Reclaiming the Training of Preachers*, can be found on Amazon: https:// www.amazon.com/dp/1720355398/ref=cm_sw_r_cp_api_i_ jG1ZCb6C2X5AA.

Chapter 4
Understanding Affirmation

1. Shad Helmstetter, *What to Say When You Talk to Yourself* (New York: Gallery Books, 2017), 26–27.
2. "Brain Stem," Centre for Neuro Skills, accessed June 10, 2019, https://www.neuroskills.com/brain-injury/brain-stem/.

Chapter 5
Loving and Being Loved

1. Tara Parker-Pope, "How to Be Better at Stress," *New York Times*, accessed June 6, 2019, https://www.nytimes.com/guides/well/how-to-deal-with-stress.
2. Benedict Carey, "Evidence That Little Touches Do Mean So Much," *New York Times*, February 22, 2010, https://www.nytimes.com/2010/02/23/health/23mind.html.
3. Carey, "Evidence That Little Touches Do Mean So Much."
4. Joseph Mattera, *An Anthology of Essays on Cutting Edge Leadership* (CreateSpace, 2015), 92–94. For more on the concepts presented, read *The Transforming Mission* by David J. Bosch, pages 36–39.
5. Mattera, *An Anthology of Essays on Cutting Edge Leadership*, 61.

Chapter 6
Unleashing Others' Potential

1. Martin B. Copenhaver, *Jesus Is the Question* (Nashville: Abingdon Press, 2014).
2. F. John Reh, "Pareto's Principle or the 80/20 Rule," The Balance Careers, updated March 22, 2019, https://www.thebalancecareers.com/pareto-s-principle-the-80-20-rule-2275148.
3. Margaret Hunter, "When and How Did the Twelve Apostles Die?," Amazing Bible Timeline With World History, April 29, 2013, https://amazingbibletimeline.com/blog/q6_apostles_die/.

Chapter 8
The Power of Failure

1. Reuben Frank, "Nick Foles' Inspirational Message in a Social Media World," NBCUniversal Media, LLC, February 5, 2018, https://www.nbcphiladelphia.com/news/sports/csn/eagles/Nick_Foles__inspirational_message_in_a_social_media_world-472769823.html.
2. "Abraham Lincoln Overcoming Failure," ChampionshipCoachesNetwork.com, accessed June 12, 2019, https://www.championshipcoachesnetwork.com/public/426.cfm.

Chapter 9
The Power of Delegation

1. Bible Hub, s.v. *"apostelló,"* accessed June 12, 2019, https://biblehub.com/greek/649.htm.
2. Bible Hub, s.v. *"apo,"* accessed June 12, 2019, https://biblehub.com/greek/575.htm.
3. Study Light, s.v. *"stéllō,"* accessed June 12, 2019, https://www.studylight.org/lexicons/greek/4724.html.
4. Bible Hub, s.v. *"dunamis,"* accessed June 12, 2019, https://biblehub.com/str/greek/1411.htm.
5. Frederick William Danker and Walter Bauer, *A Greek-English Lexicon of the New Testament and Other Early Christian Literature* (Chicago: University of Chicago Press, 2000), 278.
6. Danker and Bauer, *A Greek-English Lexicon of the New Testament and Other Early Christian Literature*, s.v. *"exousian."*

Chapter 10
The Power of Prioritizing

1. "The Pareto Principle," Natrainner, March 26, 2018, https://natrainner.wordpress.com/2018/03/26/the-pareto-principle/.

Chapter 11
The Power of Community

1. After Jerusalem was destroyed, the church was made up primarily of Gentile believers who, in their attempt to reach those in Hellenistic society, individualized Scripture to appeal to those influenced by Greek philosophy who were searching for the perfect man more than a faith community.
2. I do not believe this is referring to institutional or organizational unity but unity that comes from being in one heart and one mind—that is to say, emotional and spiritual unity. See Acts 1:14; 2:1; 2:44–46; 4:32 for an example of believers coming together as one heart, one mind, and one soul.

Chapter 13
Understanding Struggle

1. Samuel Chad, *Leadership Pain: The Classroom for Growth* (Nashville: Thomas Nelson, 2015).

Chapter 15
Understanding Spiritual Authority

1. For information on Christ Covenant Coalition, visit www. christcovenantcoalition.org.

Chapter 17
Ending Well

1. For instance, Joe Paterno's passivity regarding Jerry Sandusky that ruined his legacy at Penn State University (Sara Ganim, "CNN Exclusive: Joe Paterno May Have Known of Earlier Jerry Sandusky Abuse Claim, Police Report Reveals," Cable News Network, September 11, 2017, https://www.cnn.com/2017/09/09/us/penn-state-paterno-sandusky-police-report/index.html).

Appendix
Effective Ways to Help Mature Christ Followers

1. See Deuteronomy 31; Joshua 24; 1 Samuel 12; Matthew 5–7; and Acts 20:17–34. These scriptures are all amazing when it comes to imbuing leadership values, standards, and examples for mentors to follow.

About the Author

Dr. Joseph Mattera is an internationally known author, consultant, and scholar whose mission is to influence leaders who influence culture. He is the founding pastor of Resurrection Church and leads several organizations, including The US Coalition of Apostolic Leaders and Christ Covenant Coalition. Dr. Mattera is the author of eleven popular books, including his latest book, *Poisonous Power: Cultivating Healthy Influence in an Age of Toxic Leadership*, and is renowned for applying Scripture to contemporary culture. To order his books or to join the many thousands who subscribe to his newsletter, go to www.josephmattera.org.

Additional teachings and resources by
Dr. Joseph Mattera can be found at
www.josephmattera.org.

Audio:
https://soundcloud.com/josephmattera

Other books by Joseph Mattera—available
for purchase on Amazon:
Kingdom Revolution
Kingdom Awakening

Ruling in the Gates
Walk in Generational Blessings
Understanding the Wineskin of the Kingdom
An Anthology of Essays on Apostolic Leadership
An Anthology of Essays on Cutting Edge Leadership
Travail to Prevail
25 Truths You Never Heard in Church
The Divided Gospel
Poisonous Power

Connect with Dr. Joseph Mattera at any of the following locations:

740 40th Street
Brooklyn, New York 11232 USA
718-436-0242, ext. 13
info@josephmattera.org

Facebook: /josephmattera
Twitter: /josephmattera
YouTube: /josephmattera
Instagram: /joseph_mattera